D1174441

UNRAVELING GENDER

UNRAVELING GENDER

The Battle Over Sexual Difference

JOHN S. GRABOWSKI

TAN Books
Gastonia, North Carolina

Unraveling Gender: The Battle Over Sexual Difference
© 2022 John S. Grabowski

All rights reserved. With the exception of short excerpts used in critical review, no part of this work may be reproduced, transmitted, or stored in any form whatsoever, without the prior written permission of the publisher. Creation, exploitation and distribution of any unauthorized editions of this work, in any format in existence now or in the future— including but not limited to text, audio, and video—is prohibited without the prior written permission of the publisher.

Excerpts from the English translation of the *Catechism of the Catholic Church*, Second Edition, © 1994, 1997, 2000 by Libreria Editrice Vaticana–United States Catholic Conference, Washington, D.C. All rights reserved.

Unless otherwise noted, Scripture texts in this work are taken from the *New American Bible, revised edition* © 2010, 1991, 1986, 1970 Confraternity of Christian Doctrine, Washington, D.C. and are used by permission of the copyright owner. All Rights Reserved. No part of the New American Bible may be reproduced in any form without permission in writing from the copyright owner.

Cover design by www.davidferrisdesign.com

Cover image: Adam and Eve, 1528 (oil on panel)/Cranach, Lucas, the Elder (1472-1553)/ German/Galleria degli Uffizi, Florence, Tuscany, Italy/Bridgeman Images.

Library of Congress Control Number: 2021950427

ISBN: 978-1-5051-1719-6
Kindle ISBN: 978-1-5051-1720-2
ePUB ISBN: 978-1-5051-1721-9

Published in the United States by
TAN Books
PO Box 269
Gastonia, NC 28052
www.TANBooks.com

Printed in the United States of America

For our grandchildren

Contents

Acknowledgments   *ix*

Introduction   1

Chapter One: The Beacons Are Lit:
         Warnings about Gender Ideology   12
  A Different Kind of Battle
  The Culture of Death
  The Warnings

Chapter Two: Through the Looking Glass:
         Gender Ideology, Language, and Culture   29
  The Multiplication of Genders
  Misguided Medicine
  Purple Unicorns, Drag Queen Story Time,
    and Disney: Education or Indoctrination?
  The Language Police and the Policing of Language
  The Abolition of Man and Woman
  The Babel Effect

Chapter Three: Engendering Discussion:
         The Philosophical Roots   62
  The Dissolution of Nature, Being, and Sex
  A Marxist Vision of Gender Liberation
  Broken Cisterns, Poisoned Wells

Chapter Four: Three Revolutions   79
    The Industrial Revolution
    The Sexual Revolution
    The Technological Revolution
    Covenant Fidelity in a Fallen World

Chapter Five: Dead Ends and Detours   103
    The Gnostic Temptation
    Gender Ideology as Gnosticism
    The Dead End of Gender Ideology
    Other Detours: The Shadow of the Archetypes
    Beyond the Binary: Over the Rainbow
    Discerning Difference

Chapter Six: Beholding the Mystery:
           Receiving the Gift of Sexual Difference   132
    Sexual Complementarity
    The Spousal Meaning of the Body
    Fatherhood and Motherhood
    Nature versus Person
    Sex and Gender: Vocations, Gifts, and Roles
    Intersex Persons and the Vocation to Love
    Reading the Body

Chapter Seven: The Battle and Beyond   167
    "The Long Defeat"
    The Limits of Tolerance
    A Different Kind of War; Different Kinds of Weapons
    The Field Hospital of the Church

ACKNOWLEDGMENTS

Many people have contributed to my understanding of sexual difference informed by the light of faith over the years. Fr. Francis Martin and Fr. Donald Keefe, S.J., were formative in my days as a student—the former taught me how to read Scripture—the latter directed my doctoral dissertation. During my graduate studies, I also formed friendships with people who have been sounding boards and dialogue partners through the years, such as Scott Hahn, Chris Thompson, and, particularly, Larry Welch. Others, who have been conversation partners (whether in actual conversation or through their written work), more recently include Sr. Prudence Allen, R.S.M., Michael Waldstein, Angela Franks, Jennifer Miller, Deborah Savage, John Finley, D.C. Schindler, and David Cloutier. I have also learned from the work of many of my former students over the years on this topic: Christopher Klofft, Sarah Bartel, Christopher Gross, Fr. Thomas Petri, O.P., Fr. Christian Raab, O.S.B., and Beth Lofgren. I am particularly grateful to Pope St. John Paul II, whose vision of the human person as male and female deeply informs this book. Some of the ideas and insights in this book were first developed in a paper that I published as "Sexual Difference and the Catholic Tradition: Challenges and Resources" in *Nova et Vetera*, 19:1 (2021). I am grateful to Matthew Levering and Fr. Thomas Joseph

White, O.P., the journal's editors, for granting me permission to reuse some of that material.

Many people assisted with this book during the stages of its composition. I am particularly grateful to Claire Grabowski, Dan Grabowski, Rae Grabowski, Fr. Christian Huebner, and Christopher Klofft for helpful comments and feedback on this manuscript. I am once again thankful for the wonderful people at TAN Books who welcomed this project from its inception and offered their support and encouragement along the way, particularly John Moorehouse (the acquisitions editor who sadly passed away during the writing of this book), Patrick O'Hearn (who ably stepped into John's position and has been a wonderful resource), Conor Gallagher (the publisher), and my son Paul Grabowski (senior director of administration and technology at TAN Books), who first suggested the idea a few years ago and who enthusiastically supported it once I proposed the idea. In 2019, my wife and I wrote a book on raising Catholic children, which TAN Books published. Because of my experiences with the wonderful people at TAN Books, I wanted to publish with them again.

INTRODUCTION

Some thirty-four years ago, I was a graduate student in search of a dissertation topic. I had been captivated by Pope St. John Paul II's vision of the human person articulated in his Theology of the Body catecheses and elsewhere in his teaching. But I was not sure how a dissertation focused solely on his work would position me for the always contentious academic job market. My wife and I had two children, and my meager stipend as a graduate assistant, even when supplemented by janitorial work at a Catholic hospital, did not go very far. My wife, Claire, had begun to ask when we could expect me to get a "real job." Clearly, some prudence was required.

After much discussion with faculty and fellow doctoral students in Marquette's program in theology, I decided to write a survey dissertation focused on the question of the human person and sexual difference. The title, cumbersome as only academic works can be, was "Theological Anthropology and Gender since Vatican II: A Critical Appraisal of Recent Trends in Catholic Theology." This enabled me to focus on John Paul II's vision of the human person without neglecting the broader theological topics, including those feminist thinkers who raised the important questions and shaped much of the discussion on sexual difference in recent decades.

As we will see in this book, it was from feminist thought that the distinction between "gender" and "sex" entered into cultural conversation in the latter part of the twentieth century, though its roots are older. And yet, feminism has many flavors and faces. Even some of the pioneers of "the second wave" of the women's movement that arose in the 1960s and 70s have expressed dismay over the way feminism was hijacked by the ideology of the Sexual Revolution, deconstructed by postmodern impulses, or brought into alignment with the efforts of activists seeking to explode the idea that there are only two sexes—male and female. We will address some of this history later in the book.

Arriving at the Catholic University of America (CUA) in Washington, D.C., in the fall semester of 1991, I defended my dissertation and then worked to get tenure. At the time, the prevailing wisdom at CUA was that publishing a dissertation did not contribute to this effort since it was part of getting a degree—not part of a publication record that could count toward tenure. So, other than the mandatory publication on University Microfilms International, I did not publish my dissertation research. Instead, my writing efforts concentrated on other moral theology topics, such as marriage, family, and sexuality. Revisiting and publishing my dissertation research sat on my "to do" list for years. During that time, I remained interested in the subject of sexual difference by teaching graduate seminars, directing dissertations, and writing occasional academic articles on the topic. But then changes in the culture caught my attention.

In June 2015, the U.S. Supreme Court ruled in *Obergefell v. Hodges*, 576 U.S. 644, that laws prohibiting marriage between same-sex couples violated the due process and equal protection clauses of the Fourteenth Amendment to the U.S. Constitution. I was surprised by the sweeping nature of the ruling—but not wholly so. As I would tell my students, this was the high court's attempt to catch up to the wider culture, which had for decades excluded fertility (through widespread contraception) and permanence (through easily obtained divorce) from the lived reality of marriage. So conceived, marriage is a public declaration of love between individuals for some length of time which grants a legally recognized status and certain rights and responsibilities. It has no necessary connection to an unbreakable covenant between a man and woman ordered to the gift of children. Therefore, it has no necessary link to being male and female. And, as Chief Justice Roberts noted in his dissent to the decision, in this understanding of marriage, there is no reason why more than two adults could not enter into such a union. The Supreme Court's ill-fated decision thus opened the way for polyamorous unions comprised of three or more individuals as our vision of marriage continues to come unmoored from its Judeo-Christian roots in the doctrine of creation.[1] The chickens hatched by the Sexual Revolution have started to come home to roost.

What I did not see as clearly at that point was the ongoing dissolution of the very concept of sexual difference brought about by that same revolution. Yet, the evidence for this

---

[1]   For this point in his critique of the Court's ruling (in which Justices Scalia and Thomas joined), see pp. 20–21 of his dissent, available at https://www.supremecourt.gov/opinions/14pdf/14 -556_3204.pdf.

further impact continues to emerge. The tide of activism
that pushed *Obergefell* through the nation's high court did
not subside with winning "the right to marry" for same-sex
couples. Instead, even before that decision was rendered,
it shifted focus. Even while the debate was unfolding over
same-sex marriage, transgender issues and rights increasingly
took center stage. State and local governments and corpo-
rations found themselves caught up in "bathroom wars" as
self-identified transgender persons sought to use facilities
that corresponded with the sex with which they identified
instead of their biological or (as some called it) "assigned"
sex. Pundits and commentators spoke of a "transgender
moment" for the wider culture.[2] Instead of focusing on the
"LGB" in LGBTQ+ rights, now the focus moved on to the
"T" and the "+" (i.e., transgender and non-binary expressions of sexual difference). We were increasingly told that
a sexual binary of "male" and "female" could not accommodate the rainbow of diverse forms of sexuality shining
through the human community and the natural world. And
therefore, tragically, it must be abandoned.

In the course of writing this book, the Supreme Court,
in *Bostock v. Clayton County*,[3] delivered yet another blow to
the meaning and goodness of sexual difference in our

---

[2]   Slightly over a year before the *Obergefell* decision, *Time* magazine
proclaimed that "a transgender tipping point" had been reached.
See vol. 183, no. 22 (June 9, 2014). Twenty-two years earlier, the
same publication trumpeted emerging scientific evidence on the
biologically innate character of sex difference, asking, on its cover,
"Why are men and women different?" See vol. 139, no. 3 (January
20, 1992).

[3]   *Bostock v. Clayton County*, 140 S. Ct. 1731 (2020); available at
www.supremecourt.gov/opinions/19pdf/17-1618_hfci.pdf.

culture. While ostensibly aimed at protecting persons who have same-sex attraction or who identify as transgender from discrimination in the workplace by extending Title VII protections of the 1964 Civil Rights Acts to them, the ruling will have far-reaching implications in areas such as housing, education, and health care. Critics were quick to point out that the decision represented legislating from the bench, that it poses a significant threat to religious freedom, that it will undermine women's sports, and that it could jeopardize women's safety in public spaces such as restrooms or locker rooms.[4] These concerns have merit and will be treated in the following chapters. Once again, the high court's decision reflects the growing disconnect between sex and gender in the wider culture. It seems that the Court increasingly functions as a cultural mirror rather than simply an interpreter of law.

In addition to witnessing this continued evolution of activism in the culture, as reflected in these recent Supreme Court decisions, this further cultural development, combined with the experience of taking part in three meetings, helped shape some of my thoughts on the erosion of the concept of sexual difference. The first of these meetings was the 2015 Synod of Bishops on the Family at the Vatican, during which I served as one of the English-speaking experts. Listening to bishops from around the world describe the negative impacts of gender ideology in their dioceses helped me see the pressing pastoral as well as theological nature of the problems caused by these ideas. Further, in talking to many

---

[4]   See Ibid. Justice Samuel Alito, in his long dissenting opinion (in which Justice Thomas joined), mentioned most of these concerns.

of these same bishops, I learned that they felt hard-pressed for resources to help offer a positive and substantive response to some of these issues rather than simply echoing warnings sounded by the Holy See. In fact, Archbishop Richard Smith of Edmonton, Canada, took me to lunch so that we could discuss gender theory and ideology in hopes of broadening his knowledge on the topic. As we will discuss later in the book, when Pope Francis promulgated his Apostolic Exhortation *Amoris laetita* in early 2016, it was clear that he heard his brother bishops' concerns on this matter and took them seriously.

The second event occurred in April of 2018 in anticipation of the fiftieth anniversary of Pope St. Paul VI's watershed encyclical *Humanae vitae*. Two years earlier, I had been seated at a conference table in the United States Conference of Catholic Bishops (USCCB) offices in Washington, D.C., for a meeting of the Laity, Marriage, Family Life, and Youth Committee on which I served as a theological advisor. The idea of doing a conference for the document's anniversary was being discussed, and the consensus of the bishops at the table was clear: "We have to do this."

At that moment, I chimed into the conversation: "And it has to be at the Catholic University of America."

The bishops looked at one another, and then looked back to me with all their heads nodding in agreement: "Yes, it does."

Fifty years earlier, my university had been a locus of dissent against Paul VI's reaffirmation of the Church's teaching against contraception. When I presented the idea of hosting the conference to our university president, John Garvey, I

told him that if there is such a thing as "institutional penance," this was a chance for CUA to do it. Helping to plan
this historic conference and listening to the presentations
by theologians, philosophers, social scientists, lawyers, medical doctors, and others helped me connect more of the dots
between the rejection of God's gift of fertility and the crum-
bling of the concept of sexual difference in western culture.[5]

The third event was the annual meeting of the Academy
of Catholic Theology in May of 2019. Serving as the group's
president that year, I was given the task of planning the conference. Thinking of my experience at the synod and desir-
ing more theological reflection and resources for bishops on
this matter, I chose the theme of "Sexual Difference in the
Catholic Tradition." Again, the rich discussion and array of
high-quality papers helped me to see the deeper importance
of sexual difference in God's plan as revealed in Scripture
and elaborated in the Catholic Tradition. In turn, Sacred
Scripture and Sacred Tradition shed light on the destruction
caused by separating fertility and the male/female differences
from the human person's identity.

Unlike the Catholic vision of seeing the sexually differentiated body as an integral expression of who we are as
persons, our contemporary culture views it increasingly as
a "surface" or "screen" on which to write self-constructed
identities or currently held desires.[6]

---

[5]   These papers are available in the volume *Humanae Vitae, 50 Years
       Later: Embracing God's Vision for Marriage, Love, and Life; A Com-
       pendium*, Theresa Notare, ed. (Washington, D.C.: CUA Press,
       2019).
[6]   This idea was developed in an excellent paper given at the meet-
       ing by Angela Franks, entitled "The Body as Grid or Window:

Having attended these Catholic events and having witnessed the further unraveling of sexual difference in law and culture, I realized that now was the perfect time to return to my dissertation subject written some three decades ago. What seemed timely then seems urgent now. And the topic is not just important for theologians and academics; it is vital for anyone living in our culture who wants to think about sexual difference from a Christian perspective and understand what is at stake in the current debates.

In addition to my theology background, I have certainly benefited from reading historians and social scientists, as well as those in the "hard sciences," and I draw on that reading in framing the issues here. And, despite my background in this area, this book is neither definitive nor exhaustive. It is certainly not aimed at providing a scientific or public policy treatment of these contentious issues. There are works that cover much of this terrain effectively.[7] Instead, this book

---

A Theological Appraisal of Contemporary Aesthetics" (May 23, 2019). The paper was published as "Deleuze, Balthasar, and John Paul II on the Aesthetics of the Body" in the journal *Theological Studies*, 81, no. 3 (2020): 649–70.

[7] For an introduction to the topic that seeks to build bridges between an Evangelical Christian perspective and modern psychology see Mark Yarhouse, *Understanding Gender Dysphoria: Navigating Transgender Issues in a Changing Culture* (Downers Grove, IL: IVP Academic, 2015). Yarhouse's treatment has a neutral tone but lacks a coherent anthropology and refuses to rule out hormonal or surgical transitioning procedures in treating gender dysphoria. For an account of the history, current issues, and disputed questions regarding transgender identity, which includes perspectives from proponents and critics of gender theory, see James K. Beilby and Paul Rhodes Eddy, "Understanding Transgender Identities: An Introduction" in *Understanding Transgender Identities* (Grand Rapids: Baker Academic, 2019), 1–54. For a critique of the scien-

provides ways to think about the rich reality of sexual difference from Scripture and Catholic Tradition. Certainly, sexual difference can be viewed through other lenses that are in harmony with Christianity. I will refer to some in passing.

At the same time, there are also ways of thinking about sexual difference that are at odds with Scripture and Catholic Tradition. Unfortunately, these ideas are sowing confusion in the wider culture. There are also well-intentioned but less helpful avenues in thinking about differences between the sexes that lead ultimately to dead ends. This book will briefly address these points. However, this book's main focus centers on what the Church has come to call "gender ideology." While gender ideology has multiple origins, some from long ago, its impact today has accelerated because of large cultural shifts. Ultimately, gender ideology is best understood as a modern expression of Gnosticism, the ancient heresy that opposes Christian conceptions of creation, the Incarnation, the body, and sexual difference.

Even though *Unraveling Gender* confronts this recycled heresy by pointing out its errors, this book's primary purpose is to be explanatory. This book aims to explain what gender ideology is, where it came from, and how Scripture and the teaching of the Church offer us a better vision. Occasionally,

---

tific claims that have been advanced on behalf of gender ideology, see Paul McHugh and Lawrence S. Mayer, "Sexuality and Gender: Findings from the Biological, Psychological, and Social Sciences," *The New Atlantis,* 50 (Fall 2016): 10–143. For a critique from a legal and public policy perspective that is noteworthy for being fair and charitable to opposing views, see Ryan T. Anderson, *When Harry Became Sally: Responding to the Transgender Moment* (New York: Encounter, 2019).

I will draw on my own experience as a Catholic educator, husband, father, and grandfather when explaining ideas to make them more accessible and understandable rather than argue with anecdotal evidence.

Finally, there are some relatively new questions posed by more recent scientific research that have been intensified by the cultural upheaval that we are just beginning to grapple with and think through—the causes of sexual attraction, the phenomenon of persons whose expression of sexual difference is ambiguous on some level (i.e., intersex persons or those with disorders of sexual development), and the best ways to respond to persons who experience the pain of gender dysphoria. To these issues, my responses will be less formalized, but the witness of Scripture and the Catholic Tradition, as well as existing scientific evidence, will provide a clear framework to handle these topics in a charitable and pastoral way. Charity is crucial to those wrestling with these issues and to those seeking to understand and accompany them.

Many people are seeking answers to this pressing issue of our time—gender ideology—brought to the forefront by our current cultural turmoil. Therefore, I hope this book will provide a clearer understanding of how Scripture and Tradition can provide believers with more clarity in a confused world.

The title of the book speaks of "unraveling gender." It should be evident now that those words are used in two senses—the "unraveling" of a coherent and shared understanding of sexual difference in the wider culture and the effort to explain and demystify a complex and confusing topic in the light of both reason and faith. The book focuses more on the first of these but always with the second in view.

The Church's long history teaches us that every challenge that Christianity has faced is also an opportunity. In this case, our current cultural deconstruction of marriage, sexual difference, and the body is an opportunity to appreciate more deeply and share with greater charity God's plan for love, life, and marriage, involving male and female who together are in His image (see Gn 1:27).

Washington, D.C.
July 26, 2021
Feast of Saints Joachim and Anne

CHAPTER ONE

THE BEACONS ARE LIT: WARNINGS ABOUT GENDER IDEOLOGY

"On Shadowfax! We must hasten. Time is short. See! The bea-
cons of Gondor are alight, calling for aid. War is kindled. See,
there is the fire on Amon Dîn, and the flame on Eilenach; and
there they go speeding west; Nardol, Erelas, Min-Rimmon,
Calenhad, and the Halifirien on the borders of Rohan."[1]

—Gandalf the White, The Return of the King

The wizard Gandalf says these words at the beginning of the third volume of J.R.R. Tolkien's *Lord of the Rings* trilogy. Gandalf is here addressing his great horse Shadow-fax as he and Pippin the hobbit ride to war in Minas Tirith, Gondor's main surviving city. The people of Gondor lit great fires atop some of the flanking White Mountains to warn of the impending attack by the forces of Mordor and to implore its neighbor and ally, Rohan, to send aid for the coming battle. These beacons thus functioned as an alarm system for the peoples of Middle Earth.

---

[1] J. R. R. Tolkien, *The Return of the King* (New York: Ballantine Books, 1965), 20.

In recent years, the Church has sounded, with increasing force, a series of warnings concerning "an ideology of gender." This term describes a set of ideas that challenge and undermine basic Christian beliefs about the human person: male and female, made in the image of God, the goodness of the body, and the importance of marriage and family. Gender ideology is not, as some have suggested, "nonsense" that has "no clear referent."[2] It is very real and poses a formidable threat to the Faith and to human flourishing.

In many ways, these warnings are like the lighting of the beacons on the White Mountains—they announce the coming battle and call for aid—from both those inside of the Church and those of goodwill outside of her. In this case, the battle is not against corrupted human beings and an array of evil creatures such as orcs and trolls as in Tolkien's mythology, but against a set of ideas antithetical to human dignity and flourishing. The battle for the soul of our age is being fought—not on the fields of the Pelennor—but on the terrain of ideas about family, marriage, and sexual difference.

A Different Kind of Battle

Before proceeding, it is worth thinking more fully about the nature of this "battle"—what it is, and what it is not. The opponents in the battle are not people who identify as LGBTQ+. Tragically, such persons have been and continue to be targets of rejection, discrimination, persecution, and even overt violence within our society—at times by members of their own families or church communities. This

---

2   This is the view of Daniel Walden, "Gender, Sex, and Other Non-sense," *Commonweal*, 148, no. 3 (March 8, 2021).

hostility, along with more subtle forms of rejection, often leads to depression or other mental health issues for such persons. Meghan DeFranza describes the problems facing people who identify as transgender:

> Fifty-seven percent have family members who refuse to speak to them, 50–54 percent experience harassment at school, 60 percent have been refused health care by physicians, 64–65 percent have suffered physical or sexual violence, 57–70 percent have been discriminated against/or victimized by law enforcement, and 69 percent have experienced homelessness. Even more harrowing are the suicide rates. In the general population, the 4.6 percent rate of suicide attempts is deeply troubling, but this rate is more than double (10–20 percent) for lesbian, gay, and bisexual persons, and skyrockets to 41–46 percent for transgender and gender nonconforming people. For gender nonconforming and transgender people of color, the rate is terrifyingly high: 54–56 percent.[3]

To respond with abuse or violence toward persons with same-sex attraction or struggling with their gender identity

---

[3]   Meghan DeFranza, "Good News for Gender Minorities" in *Understanding Transgender Identities*, James K. Beilby and Paul Rhodes Eddy, eds., (Grand Rapids: Baker Academic, 2019),156–57; see also pp. 147–78. While I disagree with some of DeFranza's overall conclusions here and elsewhere, the statistics that she cites are sobering and important in recognizing the scope and gravity of the problem. It is not clear whether these numbers are adjusted to account for other forms of psychological problems or distress from which these individuals might be suffering.

is morally wrong and deserves unequivocal condemnation.[4] Further, the Church teaches that "every sign of unjust discrimination in their regard should be avoided,"[5] so the basic human rights of these persons should be protected by law, public policy, and by their neighbors.

Many persons who might describe themselves as LGBTQ+ have no desire to advance a particular political or social agenda—they simply want to live their lives in peace and without harassment from others. Those who are Christian also hope to find in their churches support in living out their call to follow Christ, while also contending with the experience of same-sex attraction or gender dysphoria. Some of these people might describe themselves as "gay," "lesbian," "queer," or "transgender."[6] Some might reject these terms as reductive and simply speak about their experience of same-sex attraction or gender discordance. The *Catechism* notes

---

4   Congregation for the Doctrine of the Faith (CDF), *Letter to the Bishops of the Catholic Church on the Pastoral Care of Homosexual Persons* (October 1, 1986), no. 10.

5   *Catechism of the Catholic Church* (*CCC*), 2358. The remark is made concerning persons who experience same-sex attraction, but the same anthropological and moral principles hold for those with gender dysphoria as well. The language of "unjust discrimination" is crucial in understanding the Church's teaching in this area. The Church believes that it is just to hold that marriage involves a covenant between one man and one woman or that the sexually differentiated body is an integral part of one's identity as a human person.

6   See for example the thoughtful presentations of Joshua Gonnerman, "Why I Call Myself a Gay Christian," *First Things* (May 23, 2012): https://www.firstthings.com/web-exclusives/2012/05/why-i-call-myself-a-gay-christian; and Eve Tushnet, "The Name of the Miracle of the Rose," Eve Tushnet, May 1, 2012 – June 1, 2012, eve-tushnet.blogspot.com.

that the pain and difficulty of such an experience can be an opportunity for these believers to unite themselves to the Cross of Christ and so to grow in holiness.[7] Like any form of suffering met with faith and love, this particular struggle can bear fruit and become a gift in the life of the individual Christian and in the wider Church community. But to acknowledge the miraculous ability of God's grace to bring good out of suffering and pain is not a license to inflict still more suffering through mistreatment. Christians are called to respond with "respect, compassion, and sensitivity"[8] to the suffering of their same-sex attracted or gender dysphoric brothers and sisters.

Yet, there are those—both inside and outside of the group of persons who identify as LGBTQ+—who have a political and social agenda aimed at deconstructing or exploding what they see as an oppressive gender binary. These proponents of gender ideology often use their positions of influence in government, the media, academia, or the culture to advance their views and to silence those who question or disagree with them. These activists, however, are ultimately not the opponents in this battle to which the Church's warnings draw our attention. Rather, it is the ideas that they promote and disseminate, and the spiritual roots of these ideas, that are the primary opponents in this battle. In a Christian context, the language of warfare always has a spiritual referent. Our battle is against the powers of evil—sin and the devil—in ourselves, and in the world around us (see Eph 6:10–17). Other human beings are not the real enemy in this battle.

---

[7]   See *CCC*, 2358.

[8]   *CCC*, 2358.

Gender ideology's ideas and views of the human person are antithetical to both human reason and Christian faith. When implemented, they work to undermine the goodness of the human body, the reality of sexual difference, the distinctive gifts of men and women, sexual complementarity, the connection between marriage and the gift of children, and the irreplaceable nature of the family as the basis of a healthy human society. When these goods are threatened, all the members of society suffer and their ability to flourish is jeopardized.

The nature and origin of these ideas will be made clearer in the pages that follow, but, for now, two things should be evident. First, the language and imagery of a "battle" used in this book or in the Church's teaching is in no way an invitation to hostility, animosity, or violence against human beings—even against the most strident advocates of gender ideology. These individuals are made in the image and likeness of God and are offered redemption in Christ, and they too have the same human dignity and value as all other persons. They deserve to be treated with respect and charity, even in the midst of debate and disagreement aimed at refuting their ideas. Second, the Church holds that her members are called to speak out against these false views of the human person precisely because of her commitment to the dignity of the human person. To fail to do so would be an abdication of the Church's responsibility. The justice and charity that we owe to others is grounded in and demands the truth— the full truth about the human person as made and loved by God. Because she has received the truth of Revelation, the

Church believes herself to be "an expert in humanity" and qualified to speak on behalf of the human person.[9]

The Culture of Death

The first person to use the term "expert on humanity" to describe the Church and what she possesses in her teaching was Pope St. Paul VI in a 1965 address to the United Nations.[10] The same pontiff was also the first to describe the Church's mission in the world as helping to build a "civilization of love" that he described as one characterized by the love and peace brought into the world at the sending of the Holy Spirit at Pentecost.[11] Both of these ideas were further developed in the magisterium of Pope St. John Paul II. And the latter notion would come to serve as the foundation for the warnings about gender ideology that the Church has been sounding.

The idea of a "civilization of love" appears frequently in the teaching of the Polish pope, including in many of his major documents.[12] In his 1994 Letter to Families, *Gratis-*

9   CDF, *Letter to the Bishops of the Catholic Church on the Collaboration of Man and Women in the Church and the World* (May 31, 2004), no. 1.

10   Paul VI, "Address of the Holy Father Paul VI to the United Nations Organization" (October 4, 1965); available at http://www.vatican.va/content/paul-vi/en/speeches/1965/documents/hf_p-vi_spe_19651004_united-nations.html.

11   See Paul VI, "Regina Coeli Address on Pentecost Sunday" (May 17, 1970).

12   Gerald W. Schlabach, based on the research of Ivan Kauffman, reports that John Paul II used the phrase some 208 times (and Paul VI used it 21 times). See Gerald W. Schlabach, *A Pilgrim People: Becoming a Catholic Peace Church* (Collegeville, MN: The Liturgical Press, 2019), 310, n. 16.

simam sane, he develops the idea at length. The civilization of love is founded upon the duality of male and female who are created in the image of God. It finds its center in the covenant of man and woman in marriage and their capacity to bring new human life into the world through their bodily self-gift to one another in cooperation with the plan of the Creator. The community of persons of the family in which spouses and children live in mutual love is a created reflection of the eternal communion of love among the divine Persons of the Trinity. The child who comes into the world through the self-giving love of his or her parents is not only a gift for them but for the whole of human society. The family and the civilization of love built upon it are, therefore, interdependent realities.[13]

Against this civilization of love stands another reality—an "anti-civilization"—it is the inverse of what it opposes, the shadow cast by the other's light. This anti-civilization denies the truth about the person and his or her dignity, about marriage, and about the family. Instead of persons being treated with respect and unconditional love, they are used as objects. Utilitarianism thus becomes the moral coin in this realm. Pope St. John Paul II writes: "Utilitarianism is a civilization of production and of use, a civilization of 'things' and not of 'persons', a civilization in which persons are used in the same way as things are used. In the context of a civilization of use, woman can become an object for man, children a hindrance to parents, the family an institution obstructing the freedom

---

[13]   See John Paul II, "Letter to Families, *Gratissimam sane*" (February 2, 1994), nos. 6–13.

of its members."[14] This false morality has entrenched itself in our culture. For example, it is weaponized in an educational context by so-called "safe sex" programs.[15] It reduces happiness to mere pleasure and freedom to selfish license. Such a view poses a fundamental threat to the family and to the society built upon it.

In his Encyclical Letter *Evangelium vitae,* Pope St. John Paul II returned to this contrast with new language, describing there what he called "the culture of death."[16] In this document, the danger posed by the "anti-civilization" is more clearly focused on the myriad threats to human life. In this view, the human being is constituted by performance—that is, the ability to do things like communicate or work. Freedom is simply the exercise of autonomous choice, and human society is simply an aggregate of such self-directed individuals. Human rights are merely extensions of individual autonomy and, therefore, can be denied to those who lack the ability to perform valuable functions (e.g., work, live independently, and think). The natural world and

---

[14]   Ibid., no. 13.

[15]   Pope St. John Paul II, in his "Letter to Families, *Gratissimam sane,*" no. 13, writes that "so-called 'safe sex', which is touted by the 'civilization of technology', is actually, in view of the overall requirements of the person, radically *not safe,* indeed it is extremely dangerous. It endangers both the person and the family. And what is this danger? It is *the loss of the truth about one's own self and about the family,* together with the risk of a loss of *freedom* and consequently of a loss of *love* itself." Other manifestations of the same utilitarian impulse in our culture can be witnessed in sequestering the elderly in facilities, the use of apps to participate in sexual hookups, or in the acceptance of social media platforms like OnlyFans (a sexually explicit picture-posting platform) as a legitimate way for people to make extra money.

[16]   See John Paul II, *Evangelium vitae* (March 25, 1995), nos. 10–17.

the human body are increasingly viewed as matter to be exploited for purposes of efficiency or pleasure. Morality is organized on the basis of either maximizing pleasure (hedonism) or efficiency (utilitarianism once again). Even life can be reduced to a commodity and is increasingly threatened through contraception, abortion, euthanasia, and hostility toward the weak and vulnerable. In Pope St. John Paul II's terms, gender ideology can be understood as a further sign and symptom of this "culture of death" at work in our world.

In response to a "culture of death," Pope St. John Paul II once again proposed a profoundly different view via a "culture of life." In this vision, it is being in relation (to God and other human beings) that is constitutive of human personhood. Freedom is found in the act of "entrustment" of self to others in love. Rights are grounded in the dignity of the person created by God and redeemed by Christ and cannot be taken away by the whim of a group or government. Nature is seen not as mere matter to be dominated, but as *mater* (i.e., a "mother") to be treated with reverence and stewardship.[17] Morality and freedom are founded on the truth of the human person, made in the image of God. Included in the document was Pope St. John Paul II's call for "a new feminism" that would reject "the temptation of imitating models of 'male domination', in order to acknowledge and affirm the true genius of women in every aspect of the life of society, and overcome all discrimination, violence and exploitation."[18] Among the unique gifts of women, the pope underscored women's unique openness to other persons and

---

[17] *Mater* is the Latin word for "mother." The play on words can be found in John Paul II, *Evangelium vitae*, no. 22.

[18] John Paul II, *Evangelium vitae*, no. 99.

to life, both of which are realized in a unique way in women's capacity to be mothers.[19]

The Warnings

It was during the long pontificate of Pope St. John Paul II that the Church began to sound warnings about gender ideology as she perceived the threat to the family taking shape. These warnings would build upon and solidify the pope's descriptions of the opposing civilizations or cultures at work. They were first sounded by various Vatican dicasteries. These dicasteries are congregations of the Roman curia that assist the pope in his governance of the Church.

In the year 2000, under the able leadership of Cardinal Alfonso López Trujillo, the Pontifical Council for the Family, in its document *Family, Marriage, and "De Facto" Unions*, issued this warning:

> Starting from the decade between 1960–1970, some theories (which today are usually described by experts as "constructionist") hold not only that generic sexual identity ("gender") is the product of an interaction between the community and the individual, but that this generic identity is independent from personal sexual identity: i.e., that masculine and feminine genders in society are the exclusive product of social factors, with no relation to any truth about the sexual dimension of the person. In this way, any sexual attitude can be justified, including homosexuality, and it is society

19   See John Paul II, Apostolic Letter *Mulieris dignitatem* (August 15, 1998), no. 18.

that ought to change in order to include other genders,
together with male and female, in its way of shaping
social life. The ideology of "gender" found a favor-
able environment in the individualist anthropology
of radical neo-liberalism. Claiming a similar status for
marriage and de facto unions (including homosexual
unions) is usually justified today on the basis of categories and terms that come from the ideology of "gender". In this way, there is a certain tendency to give the
name "family" to all kinds of consensual unions, thus
ignoring the natural inclination of human freedom to
reciprocal self-giving and its essential characteristics
which are the basis of that common good of humanity,
the institution of marriage.[20]

Note that, according to the document, the separation of
gender from the body and its sex opens the way to a proliferation of genders and undermines an understanding of the
necessarily heterosexual nature of marriage. From a different
vantage point than that of the promoters of an LGBTQ+
coalition, the Church too sees a confluence between issues
of sexual identity and sexual behavior. At its heart, gender

---

[20]   The Pontifical Council for the Family, *"Family, Marriage, and 'De
Facto' Unions"* (July 26, 2000), no. 8. My wife Claire and I were
blessed to serve as a member couple from the United States on
the Pontifical Council for the Family from our appointment in
2009 by Pope Benedict XVI until its dissolution by Pope Francis
in 2015. Much like my time at the 2015 Synod, it was a wonderful experience of the universality of the Church, meeting people
from many different cultures who, like us, were engaged in marriage and family ministry. We never had the opportunity to meet
Cardinal Trujillo, who died in 2008, under whom the Council
produced some of its most important documents.

ideology seeks to redefine what the body is and is for, and what it does.

A recent document by the Congregation for Catholic Education draws on the teaching of Pope Francis to describe this ideology:

> The context in which the *mission of education* is carried out is characterized by challenges emerging from varying forms of an ideology that is given the general name "gender theory", which "denies the difference and reciprocity in nature of a man and a woman and envisages a society without sexual differences, thereby eliminating the anthropological basis of the family. This ideology leads to educational programmes and legislative enactments that promote a personal identity and emotional intimacy radically separated from the biological difference between male and female. Consequently, human identity becomes the choice of the individual, one which can also change over time."[21]

Pope Francis has also frequently warned about the ongoing "ideological colonization" of the family by wealthy nations and international organizations. In his Apostolic Exhortation to young people *Christus vivit* he states: "In many poor countries, economic aid provided by some richer countries or international agencies is usually tied to the acceptance of Western views of sexuality, marriage, life or social justice.

21   Congregation for Catholic Education, *"Male and Female He Created Them": Towards a Path of Dialogue on the Question of Gender Theory in Education* (2019), no. 2, citing Francis, Apostolic Exhortation *Amoris laetitia* (2016), no. 56.

This ideological colonization is especially harmful to the young."[22]

The most profound analysis of both the roots and trajectory of this ideology, however, has been that provided by Pope Benedict XVI in his final Christmas address to the Roman Curia. Because of its substance and clarity, the relevant part of the address is worth quoting at some length:

> The attack we are currently experiencing on the true structure of the family, made up of father, mother, and child, goes much deeper. While up to now we regarded a false understanding of the nature of human freedom as one cause of the crisis of the family, it is now becoming clear that the very notion of being—of what being human really means —is being called into question. . . . [One thinks of] the famous saying of Simone de Beauvoir: "one is not born a woman, one becomes so" (*on ne naît pas femme, on le devient*). These words lay the foundation for what is put forward today under the term "gender" as a new philosophy of sexuality. According to this philosophy, sex is no longer a given element of nature, that man has to accept and personally make sense of: it is a social role that we choose for ourselves, while in the past it was chosen for us by society. The profound falsehood of

---

22 Francis, *Christus vivit* (March 25, 2019), no. 78. See Francis, "Address to Meeting with Families in Manila" (January 16, 2016). For a detailed examination of this ongoing effort, especially in the E.U. and the U.N., see the analysis provided by Gabriele Kuby, *The Global Sexual Revolution: Destruction of Freedom in the Name of Freedom* (Kettering, OH: Angelico Press, 2015).

this theory and of the anthropological revolution contained within it is obvious. People dispute the idea that they have a nature, given by their bodily identity, that serves as a defining element of the human being. They deny their nature and decide that it is not something previously given to them, but that they make it for themselves. According to the biblical creation account, being created by God as male and female pertains to the essence of the human creature. This duality is an essential aspect of what being human is all about, as ordained by God. This very duality as something previously given is what is now disputed. The words of the creation account: "male and female he created them" (Gen 1:27) no longer apply. No, what applies now is this: it was not God who created them male and female – hitherto society did this, now we decide for ourselves. Man and woman as created realities, as the nature of the human being, no longer exist. Man calls his nature into question. . . . Man and woman in their created state as complementary versions of what it means to be human are disputed. But if there is no pre-ordained duality of man and woman in creation, then neither is the family any longer a reality established by creation.[23]

---

23   Benedict XVI, "Christmas Address to the Roman Curia" (2012). Benedict originally attributed these ideas to Rabbi Gilles Bernheim, who was then the chief Rabbi of Paris, but Jean-Noël Darde (see http://archeologie-copier-coller.com/) subsequently demonstrated that much of Bernheim's address was plagiarized from a work by Fr. Joseph-Marie Verlinde, O.P., *L'idéologie du gender. Identité Reçue ou Choisie?* (Paris: Éditions Le Livre Ouvert, 2012).

Within these powerful remarks, there are many key insights, which will be unpacked later. However, several things deserve to be highlighted now that bring some of the main features of gender ideology into focus beyond the redefinition of the meaning and purpose of the body already noted above.

First, Pope Benedict XVI notes the transition we have undergone in our culture from "gender" as a cultural construct to now understanding it to be individually chosen. This is key to understanding our current situation and the multiplicity of "genders" around us. Second, the Holy Father tells us that to think of "gender" in this way is to turn it into a solvent that dissolves the concepts of a human nature and its Creator. As a result, we become our own creators, independent of God. So conceived, gender ideology can only be antithetical to the Christian Faith—or to other faiths that hold to an understanding of God the Creator. Third, by undermining God and His role as the author of the universe, the same ideology attacks the reality of the human person and his or her dignity. The fathers of the Second Vatican Council put it well: "For without the Creator the creature would disappear. For their part, however, all believers of whatever religion always hear His revealing voice in the discourse of creatures. When God is forgotten, however, the creature itself grows unintelligible."[24] The history of modern atheistic humanism bears testimony to the truth of this

---

For an overview of the controversy, see R.R. Reno, "Rabbi Gilles Bernheim's Plagiarism," *First Things* (May 13, 2013): https://www.firstthings.com/web-exclusives/2013/05/rabbi-gilles-bernheims-plagiarism.

[24] *Gaudium et spes*, no. 36.

teaching.[25] Ideological iterations of this atheistic humanism—whether from the political right or the political left—
are responsible for some of the most bloodstained chapters
of our modern history. Fourth, it is not accidental that Pope
Benedict XVI anchors his understanding of the human person in the words of Genesis 1:27: "Male and female he created them." Like Pope St. John Paul II, Pope Benedict XVI
understood the deep meaning and importance of Genesis's
opening chapters as the foundation for understanding the
human person in God's plan.

In the coming chapters, we will follow Pope Benedict's
lead in tracing the intellectual and cultural roots of this ideology in currents of modern philosophy utilized by twentieth-century feminists. We will also explore various cultural
shifts that have unleased this ideology while proposing an
alternative vision, one that returns to the biblical doctrine of
creation, But first, we must survey the terrain of the present
culture and the confusion that has enveloped basic concepts
such as male or female.

---

[25]   See the magnificent study of Henri de Lubac, S.J., *The Drama of
Atheist Humanism*, trans. Edith M. Riley, Anne Englund Nash,
and Mark Sebanc (London: Sheed and Ward, 1949; rpt. San
Francisco: Ignatius, 1995). In many ways this study underlies the
Council's analysis of the modern world and the forms of atheism
in it.

CHAPTER TWO

THROUGH THE LOOKING GLASS: GENDER IDEOLOGY, LANGUAGE, AND CULTURE

*"When **I** use a word," Humpty Dumpty said in a rather scornful tone, "it means just what I choose it to mean—neither more nor less."*

*"The question is," said Alice, "whether you **can** make words mean so many different things."*

"The question is," said Humpty Dumpty, "which is to be master—that's all."
                    —Lewis Carroll, Through the Looking Glass[1]

"Come, let us go down and there confuse their language, so that no one will understand the speech of another."
                                        —Genesis 11:7

Not long ago, the word "gender" had a very different meaning. It could refer to classes of nouns in particular languages such as French or Spanish. But, other than grammatical gender, the word was largely used as a synonym

---

[1]   Emphasis in the original.

for "sex," as in being male or female.[2] One did not say "sex" in polite company as it could be misunderstood as a reference to some form of sexual activity. Instead, one would say "gender" to describe sexual difference in order to avoid possibly giving unwitting offense. In this kind of usage, the answer to the question of how many genders there are was an easy one—two. This is because it was understood that the sexual dimorphism evident in human beings and much of the animal world reflected the binary quality of sexual difference. These observable differences pointed to basic and complementary functions in reproductive biology. Philosophers of ancient Greece pondered these functions in their descriptions of nature and human beings. Angela Franks, summarizing the monumental historical research of Sr. Prudence Allen, puts the matter succinctly:

> The ancient Greeks noticed that binary sexual generation was not reserved to humans but also was a feature of the most developed animal species. While entailing quite a bit of variation, nevertheless sexual generation that was a binary affair usually followed these parameters: approximately one-half of the species-members contributed by reproducing outside of themselves (the males), and the other half of the members by reproducing inside themselves (the females).
>
> We know now that this is because males produce spermatozoa, and females produce ova. But these

---

[2]   It is difficult to correlate sexual difference and grammatical gender. Romance languages have three grammatical genders (masculine, feminine, and neuter); others have no grammatical genders; still others more than three.

gametes contribute to reproduction outside and inside the body respectively, so the ancients were grasping things correctly, albeit partially. This division certainly holds for human beings.[3]

As Franks notes, given the sweep of human history, this was the common belief of human beings until roughly "the day before yesterday" (i.e., the late twentieth century). This view was untroubled by the existence of a small number of human beings in whom the expression of sexual difference was ambiguous—what the ancient world often called "hermaphrodites," and what we now describe as persons with intersex conditions.[4] These individuals have various genetic or hormonal conditions that impact their expression of sexual difference (external genitalia or secondary sex characteristics) or their ability to reproduce sexually (sometimes affecting the gonads or internal genitalia in addition to observable sexual characteristics). But the very term "intersex" describes someone who exists between the two sexes. The prefix *inter* comes from Latin and means "between," "among," or "in the midst of." The existence of such persons does not negate the reality of two sexes—it reinforces it. In this case, the exception confirms the rule.

Despite this history, etymology, and the observable facts of biology, some people, today, believe that there are many dozens of genders and that it is possible to have multiple

---

[3] Angela Franks, "What is a Woman?," *Catholic World Report*, March 9, 2020, https://www.catholicworldreport.com/2020/03/09/what -is-a-woman/.

[4] These conditions are also sometimes designated as disorders (or differences) of sexual development—DSDs.

genders or none at all. Pope Benedict XVI gave a concise overview of the evolution of this word in his last Christmas address to the Roman curia, and we will unpack the intellectual and cultural forces behind this evolution in the next chapter. However, before we consider how we got here, it is worth asking: "Where are we?" What follows is in no way exhaustive but is a cursory sampling of the strange new world that gender ideology is beginning to fashion among us. Like Alice having passed through the mirror in Lewis Carroll's story, the "Looking-Glass World" in which we find ourselves is strange, the language is often alien, and common sense is altogether uncommon. Rather than losing ourselves in the essential novelty of some of the individual features of the terrain,[5] we will instead try to examine some of the larger and more troubling features of this emerging world.

---

[5] For example, we could consider stories about middle-aged fathers who decide that they identify as six-year-old girls and leave their families to be "raised" by an elderly couple. See Ashley Rae Goldenberg, "Transgender AND Transager: 52 Year-Old Father Lives as a 6 Year-Old Girl," MRCTV, December 7, 2015, www.mrctv .org/blog/52-year-old-father-lives-6-year-old-girl. Or we could point to the case of a person who identifies as a transgender man who was artificially inseminated by sperm from another person who identifies as a transgender woman and gave birth to a child delivered by a transgender doctor. Now "he" and his non-binary partner are being hailed as "Britain's most modern family." See Rob Bailey-Millado, "Transgender man gives birth to baby using sperm from trans woman," The New York Post, December 30, 2019, https://nypost.com/2019/12/30/transgender-man-gives-bi rth-to-baby-using-sperm-from-trans-donor/.

The Multiplication of Genders

In November of 2019, the International Law Commission of the United Nations (U.N.) proposed a new treaty defining crimes against humanity that would officially recognize 100 different genders. This would replace the 1998 Rome Statute that identified "gender" as "man and woman in the context of society."[6] If adopted by the General Assembly, this could have a significant impact on other U.N. treaties and aid programs, potentially affecting billions of people around the world. This would mean that the U.N. would follow in the wake of popular social media platforms[7] and many in academia and the entertainment industry in adopting the view that sexual difference is merely a social construct.

This new treaty would also represent another formal step toward the U.N.'s adaptation of the so-called Yogyacarta Principles (YPs) drafted by a group of activists in 2007 and presented in Geneva that same year. Purporting to extend the language and tradition of international human rights to

---

[6]   See Stefano Gennarini, "General Assembly Inches Toward Redefining Gender as Social Construct," Center for Family and Human Rights, *Friday Fax,* vol. 22, No. 45 (November 7, 2019): https://c-fam.org/friday_fax/general-assembly-inches-toward-redefining-gender-as-social-construct/.

[7]   Facebook, for example, has held this view for years. See Rhiannon Williams, "Facebook's 71 gender options come to UK users," *The Telegraph*, June 27, 2014, http://www.telegraph.co.uk/technology/facebook/10930654/Facebooks-71-gender-options-come-to-UK-users.html. If individuals do not identify with any of these preset options, Facebook allows them to create their own. See https://www.facebook.com/facebookdiversity/posts/last-year-we-were-proud-to-add-a-custom-gender-option-to-help-people-better-expr/774221582674346/.

matters of sexual discrimination, the YPs offer the following
definition of gender identity:

> UNDERSTANDING "gender identity" to refer to
> each person's deeply felt internal and individual expe-
> rience of gender, which may or may not correspond
> with the sex assigned at birth, including the personal
> sense of the body (which may involve, if freely chosen,
> modification of bodily appearance or function by med-
> ical, surgical or other means) and other expressions of
> gender, including dress, speech and mannerisms.[8]

Thus, gender identity is, at its deepest level, a feeling
largely unrelated to "the sex assigned at birth." An identity
that this feeling creates can only be fluid. Efforts to insist
on a connection between gender identity and the body or
sexual reproduction in terms of morality or public policy is
viewed as a form of discrimination.[9]

Oddly, as author Ryan Anderson notes, some gender
activists hold both that gender identity is fixed at birth *and*
that it is completely fluid. Anderson notes a recent CNN
report on the subject that stated that gender identity and its
expression "'can change every day or even every few hours,'
and this fluidity 'can be displayed in how we dress, express,
and describe ourselves.'"[10] Yet, activist organizations such as

---

[8]   See Preamble, "The Yogyakarta Principles," https://yogyakartap
rinciples.org/preambule/. For an overview and critique of these
principles and their implications, see Kuby, *The Global Sexual Revolution*, 64–81.

[9]   Kuby, 67.

[10]   Anderson, *When Harry Became Sally*, p. 39, quoting Lauren Book-
er's CNN story "What it means to be gender-fluid," April 13,

the World Professional Association for Transgender Health, the Human Rights Campaign, and the American Civil Liberties Union argue that children as young as two to four years old can develop a gender identity discordant from that assigned at birth in which they should be affirmed and supported by parents, teachers, and medical professionals. Sounding a note of common sense, Anderson observes, "A three-year-old child is just beginning to learn the difference between boys and girls, so how could that child have any sense of really being a boy when everyone says she's a girl?"[11] In other words, the idea that a three-year-old could have a clear and fixed psychological sense of him or herself as trapped in the wrong body, when he or she is just coming to understand that body and how it differs from the other sex, seems unrealistic.

Misguided Medicine

The philosophical idea of gender as a social construct flagged by Pope Benedict XVI was introduced into the social sciences and ultimately into the field of medicine in the mid-twentieth century by psychologist John Money. For Money, gender was simply a "role" one takes on unrelated to the body, and, therefore, it could be learned and unlearned. His work was influential in creating a rationale for medical gender transitioning treatments such as surgical sex reassignment, despite being widely criticized. In fact, some of his methods can only be described as being sexually and psychologically abusive. His most famous patient, David Reamer,

2016.
[11]   See Ibid., 34–36.

was "treated" by Money and raised as a girl after a botched infant circumcision. As an adolescent and young adult, Reamer rejected this assigned gender, attempted to transition back to his biological sex, and, ultimately, committed suicide.[12] Despite his horrific methods and outcomes such as this, Money's work and the theory it founded remain influential (and often cited) within literature promoting gender ideology in the social and medical sciences.

So, what does good medical care mean for gender activists? It means that these gender discordant children should socially transition as children (meaning that they should be able to choose the clothing and name the gender pronouns with which they identify). As these children approach adolescence, they should be given puberty blockers to prevent their bodies from maturing in their biological sex. These delay puberty and serve to regress sex characteristics that have begun to manifest in childhood (decreasing breast tissue in girls and testicular volume in boys). Around sixteen years of age, these young people should receive cross-hormone therapy so that they begin to develop the secondary sex characteristics of the opposite sex. At eighteen, these individuals should be able to opt to undergo surgical transitioning that involves the surgical amputation of primary and secondary sex characteristics and cosmetic reconstruction

[12]   For an overview of Money's work and this tragic case, see Mary Farrow, "The story behind sex change surgery you haven't heard," Catholic News Agency, January 19, 2017, https://www.catholicnewsagency.com/news/35256/the-story-behind-sex-change-surgery-you-havent-heard.

of external genitalia (and possibly breast augmentation for male to female transitions).[13]

Is this good medicine? This question can be answered from an evidence-based perspective and a philosophical one. In both cases, the answer is no. Neither of these negative answers are surprising when one considers that the therapeutic recommendations put forward by proponents of gender ideology are based on a flawed view of the human person and his flourishing.

On a practical level, significant evidence indicates that these treatments are unwise and detrimental to one's health. The idea that a child has a fixed gender identity at odds with his or her body by the age of two or three is nonsensical. Children and adolescents go through considerable flux in their sense of self, and gender non-conformity is frequently one manifestation of that. Studies consistently find that between "80 and 95 percent of children who say they are transgender naturally come to accept their sex and enjoy emotional health by late adolescence."[14] Why would someone embark on the painful, extensive, and lasting form of intervention that transitioning procedures entail in the face of such numbers? This contradicts the evidence-based trend in contemporary medicine to opt for the least invasive form of treatment available. The idea of a discordant gender

---

[13]   For a detailed analysis of these procedures and their effects, see Anderson, *When Harry Became Sally*, 97–103, 120–22.

[14]   Paul R. McHugh, Paul Hruz, and Lawrence S. Mayer, Brief of *Amici Curiae* in Support of Petitioner, *Gloucester County School Board v. G.G.*, Supreme Court of the United States, No. 16-273 (January 10, 2017), 12, https://www.scotusblog.com/wp-content/uploads/2017/01/16-273-amicus-petitioner-mchugh.pdf.

identity being cemented in early childhood is further undermined by the phenomenon of what is being called "rapid
onset gender dysphoria" where adolescents or adults sud-
denly begin to identify as a member of the other sex, often
after exposure to gender ideology or a peer group impacted
by it.[15] For these reasons, it seems clear that simply wait-
ing or using some form of gender-affirming psychological
therapy for children with significant discordance is the wiser
course for children and youth.[16]

Besides supporting data, there are also practical reasons
that suggest this kind of aggressive chemical and surgical
intervention is an imprudent action for adults who suffer
from gender discordance.[17] On the physical level, it should

---

[15]   On this relatively new phenomenon, see Lisa Littman, "Peer
Group and Social Media Influences in Adolescent and Young-
Adult Rapid-Onset Gender Dysphoria," Journal of the American
Academy of Child & Adolescent Psychiatry, October 2018, Vol.
57 (10), S73-S74 and *eadem*, "Parent reports of adolescents and
young adults perceived to show signs of a rapid onset of gender
dysphoria," PlosOne 14, no. 3, https://journals.plos.org/ploso
ne/article?id=10.1371/journal.pone.0202330. For an extended
treatment, see Abigail Shrier, *Irreversible Damage: The Transgender
Craze Seducing Our Daughters* (Washington, D.C.: Regnery Publishing, 2020).

[16]   For a good overview of what this therapy involves and the ways in
which it is a safer path than that outlined by gender activists, see
Anderson, *When Harry Became Sally*, 123–44.

[17]   It is worth noting that the previous edition of the fourth edition of
the Diagnostic and Statistical Manual of Mental Disorders (DSM-
IV) described gender discordance as "gender identity disorder."
However, in the revision of this text in 2013 (DSM-5), the American Psychiatric Association renamed the condition "gender dysphoria" and recommended psychological intervention only when
this condition is associated with "clinically significant distress." See
the APA Bulletin, http://www.dsm5.org/documents/gender%20d

be noted that these procedures do not alter an individual's genetic sex, and they permanently destroy his or her fertility. A person who has fully transitioned may look like a member of the opposite sex but will never bear children as one. Individuals who have undergone transitioning procedures also experience reduced sexual function and sensation because of cosmetic reconfiguration or reconstruction of their genitalia. Further, these individuals remain at odds with their bodies' biochemistry as they will need to continue cross-sex hormonal therapy for the remainder of their lives.

From a psychological perspective, there is abundant reason for caution. Specifically, significant evidence reveals that aggressive hormonal and surgical transitioning procedures do not improve mental health outcomes for people who undergo them—even in ostensibly LGBTQ+ friendly cultures.[18] Anderson summarizes the findings conducted at the

---

ysphoria%20fact%20sheet.pdf. Critics argue that this change was based more on politics and the advocacy of gender activists than science. For an overview of this debate, see John S. Grabowski and Christopher Gross, "An Analysis of GSUSA's Policy of Serving Transgender Youth: Implications for Catholic Practice," *Journal of Moral Theology*, 5:1 (2016), 89–96; and Anderson, *When Harry Became Sally*, 94–97.

[18]   Authors of a recent widely cited study touting the mental health benefits of transitioning procedures have had to retract their claims after having them challenged by wider statistical analysis, admitting: "The results demonstrated no advantage of surgery in relation to subsequent mood or anxiety disorder-related health care visits." See Richard Bränström and John E. Pachankis, "Reduction in Mental Health Treatment Utilization Among Transgender Individuals After Gender-Affirming Surgeries: A Total Population Study," *American Journal of Psychiatry*, 177:8 (August 2020): https://ajp.psychiatryonline.org/doi/pdf/10.1176/appi.ajp .2020.1778correction.

Karolinska Institute and Gothenburg University in Sweden, one of the largest and most rigorous academic studies to date:

> The rate of psychiatric hospitalization for postoperative transsexuals was about three times the rate for the control groups, adjusted for previous psychiatric treatment. The risk of mortality from all causes was significantly higher and so was the rate of criminal conviction. Suicide attempts were nearly five times more frequent, and the likelihood of death by suicide was *nineteen* times higher—again after adjustment for prior psychiatric illness.[19]

Data such as these do not suggest that these procedures are a path to flourishing for those who undergo them—contrary to the claims of proponents of gender ideology. There is, however, significant evidence that gender dysphoria or discordance in both children and adults is better treated psychologically rather than medically.[20] In the view of many

---

For a summary and overview of more mainstream scientific findings, see Lawrence S. Meyer and Paul McHugh, "Sexuality and Gender: Findings from the Biological, Psychological, and Social Sciences," *The New Atlantis* 50, Part II (Fall 2016): https://www.thenewatlantis.com/publications/part-two-sexuality-mental-health-outcomes-and-social-stress-sexuality-and-gender. For an argument on the deep biological basis of sexual difference and identity see Debra Soh, *The End of Gender: Debunking the Myths about Sex and Identity* (New York: Threshold Editions, 2020).

[19] Anderson, *When Harry Became Sally*, 103 (emphasis in original). See also R.K. Simonsen, A. Giraldi, E. Kristensen, and G. M. Hald, "Long-Term Follow-Up of Individuals Undergoing Sex Reassignment Surgery: Psychiatric Morbidity and Mortality," *Nordic Journal of Psychiatry*, 70, no. 4 (2016): 241–47.

[20] See Richard P. Fitzgibbons, Philip Sutton, and Dale O'Leary,

doctors and psychologists, gender dysphoria is akin to other psychological conditions such as body dysmorphic disorder or anorexia. It is "a disorder of assumptions" as Paul McHugh notes.[21] Just as one would not prescribe appetite suppressants or liposuction for a person suffering from anorexia, it is a mistake to try to treat gender discordance by aggressive chemical and surgical overwriting of the person's body. What the person truly needs is help accepting their body and their self-worth—a point brought home by listening to the stories of those who have "de-transitioned" by seeking to undo (to the degree possible) the harm done to their bodies by hormonal and surgical transitioning.[22] In a particularly chilling development, some governments are moving to criminalize de-transitioning procedures or therapies aimed at helping people struggling with gender dysphoria to accept their bodies.[23]

"The Psychopathology of 'Sex Reassignment' Surgery: Assessing Its Medical Psychological, and Ethical Appropriateness," *National Catholic Bioethics Quarterly* 9, no. 1 (2009): 97–125; and Meyer and McHugh, "Sexuality and Gender," 10–143.

[21] Paul McHugh, "Transgender Surgery Isn't the Solution," *Wall Street Journal*, May 13, 2016.

[22] Anderson devotes a whole chapter to personal stories of people who have de-transitioned" after invasive gender transitioning procedures. See Anderson, "De-Transitioners Tell Their Stories," in *When Harry Became Sally,* 49–76.

[23] The Australian state of Victoria recently passed The Change or Suppression (Conversion) Practices Prohibition Bill aimed at doing just this, thereby conflating gender dysphoria and sexual attraction. See the interview with Archbishop Peter Comensoli of Melbourne in *The Pillar*, "Melbourne archbishop: LGBT conversion therapy law silences ministers, parents, and doctors," https://www.pillarcatholic.com/p/melbourne-archbishop-lgbt-conversion.

These procedures also appear problematic when we consider the nature and aims of medicine that call on physicians to use their skill to heal rather than harm.[24] Medicine does not exist to simply fulfill the desires of individuals—especially when doing so causes them demonstrable harm. Hence, Catholic moral theology and Catholic healthcare institutions oppose these practices as a form of unwarranted mutilation of healthy bodies that is not in the patient's interest and not congruent with the dignity of persons or the nature of medicine. And, therefore, a Catholic understanding of healthcare's purpose insists that healthcare is a moral enterprise, not merely a technical enterprise. Good medicine is aimed at helping human beings to flourish—physically and psychologically. Therefore, it must be based on a sound understanding of the person and of sexual difference.

Purple Unicorns, Drag Queen Story Time, and Disney: Education or Indoctrination?

Biology is hard to overcome. This reality was brought home to us when our first four children (who were born within seven years of each other) were young. We had two girls first, so most of our toys were typically designed for them. My wife and I wondered what the impact might be on our sons.

---

[24]	The Oath of Hippocrates, widely regarded as a foundational document for western medical ethics, describes a covenantal relationship between physician and patient in which the doctor swears (among other things) to use his or her skill "for the benefit of the sick according to [his or her] ability and judgment . . . [and to] keep them from harm and injustice." See William C. Shiel, Jr., "Medical Definition of Hippocratic Oath," https://www.medicinenet.com/script/main/art.asp?articlekey=20909.

The question was answered when our young boys picked up their sisters' Barbies and began to swordfight with them. The same lesson was learned on a national scale by the social engineers of the day care system in the former Soviet Union and the Israeli kibbutzim. Their efforts to collectivize child rearing and to overcome sex differences by raising children in gender neutral environments were marked failures.[25] Those failures leave proponents of gender ideology unfazed.

Proponents of gender ideology have definite views on the way in which children should be raised and educated. In some cases, parents are urged not to "assign a sex" to their children when they are born but rather to allow children to choose their own gender. These "theybies" (rather than "babies") grow up with their biological sex and its import largely hidden from them.[26] They are given gender-neutral names and their parents do their best to block any harmful "gender stereotypes" from them. No pink or blue—only endless shades of yellow or gray—even at the "gender reveal" parties of these little ones (if they were to have them). In such cases, children are being socialized into a confused gender identity.

Activists have also designed programs ostensibly to promote awareness and acceptance of transgender and self-described "gender queer" persons in educational contexts. One prime example was "the genderbread person" that sought to

---

[25] See Michael Levin, *Feminism and Freedom* (New York: Routledge, 1987), 57, 283.

[26] See for example, Julie Compton, "'Boy or girl?' Parents raising 'theybies' let kids decide," NBC News, July 19, 2018, https://www.nbcnews.com/feature/nbc-out/boy-or-girl-parents-raising-theybies-let-kids-decide-n891836.

teach children that "gender" is a complex correlation of feelings created by body awareness, self-chosen gender identity (located in the brain), gender expression, romantic attraction, and sexual attraction.[27] This version, however, was criticized by other activists because its "gingerbread man" shape was said to be too male and it used the language of "biological sex" that critics regarded as problematic. The latest iteration replaces this language with "anatomical sex" and "sex assigned at birth."[28] But because of these perceived problems, Trans Students Educational Resources (TSER) has created the "purple unicorn" image to teach the same ideas to children without any "problematic" association with either maleness or biological sex.[29] Such programs are increasingly common in the public school curriculum.

If these programs help to promote better understanding of gender discordant children, reduce bullying or violence by their peers, and encourage greater sensitivity by educators, those outcomes are certainly positive outcomes. However, it seems evident that these programs have other more important goals in mind. In fact, the images and programs aim to explain why gender should be regarded as primarily located in the brain rather than the body and why there are an endless array of genders—not two. For young children,

---

[27]   See "Gingerbread Person v3.3," The Gingerbread Person, c. 2015, https://www.genderbread.org/resource/genderbread-person-v3-3, for the visual of version 3.3.

[28]   See "Gingerbread Person v4.0," The Gingerbread Person, https://www.genderbread.org/resource/genderbread-person-v4-0.

[29]   See "Gender Unicorn," Trans Student Educational Resources, http://www.transstudent.org/gender/, for the Gender Unicorn image.

this can serve to destabilize and create doubt about their own sense of themselves, their bodies, and their gender. That is, they can create gender confusion where there was none. The growth of "rapid onset gender dysphoria" among adolescents and young people mentioned above lends credence to that possibility—exposure to ideology and peer groups can destabilize a sense of self as male or female that was previously unproblematic.

The same might be said for the "drag queen story hour" initiative adopted by many local schools, community centers, and public libraries. Here, men dressed as women (or "in drag") come in to read a story (usually about some form of sexual diversity) to a group of children. To cite the group's self-description from their website: "DQSH captures the imagination and play of the gender fluidity of childhood and gives kids glamorous, positive, and unabashedly queer role models. In spaces like this, kids are able to see people who defy rigid gender restrictions and imagine a world where people can present as they wish, where dress up is real."[30] Again, while the ostensible purpose is to promote tolerance and inclusiveness and discourage bullying of individuals who appear different, there is obviously another agenda at work—to give children "unabashedly queer role models" and to learn to "defy rigid gender restrictions." Unfortunately, this helps children accept an understanding of gender that is multiple, fluid, and queer, rather than located in any kind of binary linked to the body or to biology. And those children attending such events who have no difficulty

---

[30]   See "What is Drag Queen Story Hour?" Drag Queen Story Hour, https://www.dragqueenstoryhour.org/.

thinking of themselves as a girl or a boy might well begin to
think otherwise.

Once known as a bastion of family-friendly entertainment, these days the Walt Disney Company is also not shy
when it comes to indoctrinating our youth with gender confusion. In a recent episode of the Disney Junior Channel's
show, Muppet Babies, its male character Gonzo, attended
a ball in a princess dress under the name "Gonzo-rella."[31]
Directed at four to seven-year-olds, this messaging in the
Muppet Babies program is another sign that the transgender
agenda is getting a louder voice in the media as it seeks to
target our children.

The Language Police and the Policing of Language

A related and even more disturbing aspect of the "Looking
Glass World" shaped by gender ideology is the weaponization of language. Proponents of gender ideology insist that
people who identify as transgender have a right to select
which words and pronouns can be used to address them—
whether these be pronouns associated with the other sex,
plural pronouns (such as they, their, or them) to refer to
individuals, or a whole new set of "non-binary" pronouns
such as "ze, sie, hir, co, and ey."

This request is not always made as a matter of courtesy—
it is increasingly made with the force of policy, law, and the
threat of punishment. People who "misgender" others by
using pronouns other than those chosen by the individual

---

[31]　　See Sam Dorman, "'Muppets Babies' character crossdresses, becomes 'Gonzorella,'" August 2, 2021, https://www.foxnews.com
/entertainment/muppets-babies-gonzo-princess.

are subject not just to social ostracism but, in some cases, the threat of criminal prosecution.[32] In October of 2017, California passed a law that threatens health care workers with jail time for "misgendering" the elderly by not using their chosen forms of address.[33] In New York City, those who deliberately "misgender" others can be fined up to one quarter of a million dollars.[34] In Scandinavia, some Christians are facing criminal prosecution for articulating traditional Christian positions on same-sex sexual relationships or defending the idea that there are only two genders on the charge that such views "incite hatred."[35]

Others who fail to conform to the new language orthodoxy shaped by gender ideology suffer threats to their

---

[32]   On recent cases in the U.K., see Rachel del Guidice, "Police Question UK Journalist for 'Misgendering' a Transgender Woman," *The Daily Signal*, March 19, 2019, https://www.dailysignal.com/2019/03/19/police-question-uk-journalist-for-misgendering-a-transgender-woman/.

[33]   See Mary Rezac, "California bill seeks to punish 'misgendering' with jail time," *Crux*, September 2, 2017, https://cruxnow.com/church-in-the-usa/2017/09/02/california-bill-seeks-punish-misgendering-jail-time/. The bill, which passed in October 2017, is currently being challenged in court.

[34]   See the column by UCLA Law Professor Eugene Volokh, "You can be fined for not calling people 'ze' or 'hir,' if that's the pronoun they demand that you use," *The Washington Post*, May 17, 2016, https://www.washingtonpost.com/news/volokh-conspiracy/wp/2016/05/17/you-can-be-fined-for-not-calling-people-ze-or-hir-if-thats-the-pronoun-they-demand-that-you-use/.

[35]   Both Rev. Dr. Juhana Pohjola, Dean of the Evangelical Lutheran Mission Diocese of Finland and Dr. Päivi Räsänen, a member of the Finnish Parliament and former Minister of the Interior, have had criminal charges brought against them on these grounds. See Gene Veith, "Criminalizing Christian Teachings about Sex," February 11, 2020, https://www.patheos.com/blogs/geneveith/2020/02/criminalizing-christian-teachings-about-sex/.

livelihood. Shawnee State University in Ohio (a state-run school) instituted disciplinary action against philosophy professor Nicholas Meriwether who declined to use feminine pronouns (such as "her," or "Miss") for a male student in his course who identified as transgender. When pressed by the institution, the professor offered to use the student's first or last name and to address all other persons in the course in the same way; however, this compromise was rejected by both the student and the university that demanded compliance with the student's self-chosen pronouns. The professor believed that this coercion violated both his free speech rights and his Christian convictions. After a district court ruling sided with the university, the professor appealed to the U.S. Sixth Circuit.[36] That court reversed the district court, but Meriweather still has a way to go before he legally proves that his rights were violated.[37]

This phenomenon is not limited only to state schools. I have received calls from former students now teaching at Catholic universities seeking advice concerning their students who demand to be addressed with pronouns that do not correspond to their biological sex. If these teachers decline to do so, they find themselves, in some cases, attacked in the campus newspaper as "transphobic." This

---

[36]   For an overview of the case by the Alliance Defending Freedom who is representing the professor in the case, see "Professor appeals decision that lets Shawnee State force him to speak contrary to his beliefs," March 12, 2020, www.adfmedia.org/News/PRDetail /10842. I was one of a number of Catholic scholars who signed an amicus curiae brief in support of the professor in the case.

[37]   The Sixth Circuit's opinion is available at www.opn.ca6.uscourts .gov/opinions.pdf/21a0071p-06.pdf.

aggressive strategy of public shaming is likely to continue to spread in Catholic and other private schools.

Even previously publicly declared progressive stances on issues such as the rights of those who describe themselves as gay, lesbian, bisexual, or in support of "gay marriage" do not make one immune from attack or vilification if he or she deviates from the party line upheld by proponents of gender ideology. *Denver Post* op-ed columnist Jon Caldara was fired for arguing, in the name of transparency, that parents deserve to know what their children are learning in sex-education about multiple genders and transgender health issues.[38] This was in spite of overall "liberal" stances on social issues, writing in favor of euthanasia, gay marriage, and transgender rights. To cite Caldara's own account of the matter and his largely libertarian views:

> What seemed to be the last straw for my column was my insistence that there are only two sexes and my frustration that to be inclusive of the transgendered (even that word isn't allowed) we must lose our right to free speech. To be clear I am strongly pro-gay marriage, which has frustrated many of my socially conservative friends. I have friends, family and employees from the LGBT community. I don't care who uses whose bathroom, what you wear, or how you identify. People from this community have rights which we must protect. But to force us to use inaccurate pronouns, to

---

[38] See Madeline Kearns, "Columnist Fired for Stating Sex Is Binary," *National Review* (January 22, 2020): https://www.nationalreview.com/2020/01/transgender-politics-columnist-fired-for-stating-sex-is-binary/.

force us to teach our kids that there are more than two sexes, to call what is plainly a man in a dress, well, not a man in a dress violates our right of speech.[39]

Likewise, popular author J.K. Rowling, herself an advocate for women, self-identified gay, lesbian, bisexual people, and the safety of those who describe themselves as transgender, was subject to a backlash of people attacking her as "transphobic" for mocking a headline that contained the words "people who menstruate."[40] This earned her the pejorative title of "TERF" (or Trans Exclusionary Radical Feminist) in some quarters. Rowling explained in a subsequent blog post that she does not want those who identify as transgender to be mistreated or harmed, and she believes that transitioning can help some people. Nonetheless, she is concerned (among other things) by the growing numbers of young women seeking transitioning, the rise in "rapid onset" gender dysphoria, and (as a sexual abuse and assault survivor) the safety of women who must share public spaces (such

---

[39] John Caldara, "Here's the Column that Got me Fired from the Denver Post," January 20, 2020, available on the Independence Institute website at https://i2i.org/heres-the-column-that-got-me -fired-from-the-denver-post/. The piece also contains a link to the original column.

[40] She posted on Twitter: "'People who menstruate.' I'm sure there used to be a word for those people. . . . Someone help me out. Wumben? Wimpund? Woomud?" See Saba Hamedy, "Daniel Radcliffe responds to J.K. Rowling's tweets about gender identity," CNN, June 9, 2020, https://www.cnn.com/2020/06/08/enterta inment/daniel-radcliffe-responds-jk-rowling-trans-tweets-trnd/in dex.html. She has also been disavowed by prominent *Harry Potter* fan websites. See BBC News, "JK Rowling: Harry Potter fan sites reject author's trans comments," July 3, 2020, https://www.bbc .com/news/entertainment-arts-53276007.

as bathrooms and locker rooms) with biological males who identify as women.[41] She has also added her voice to a group of largely liberal academics, writers, and other public intellectuals who have spoken out about the danger posed by the restriction of speech in public life and debate.[42]

These last examples bring into focus one of the new features of gender ideology and other components of the contemporary intersectional politics of the left—what some refer to as "cancel culture."[43] This has become the ultimate enforcement tool for conformity to codes of politically correct language use. This practice involves a public attack on those who break with the new political orthodoxy in some way with aim of public shaming, boycotting, and getting the individuals banned from public forums or social media platforms. It can affect a person's ability to share products or ideas, especially as Big Tech and publishers take steps to censor or eliminate views that challenge the tenets of gender ideology.[44] It can also get a person fired from a job. The

---

[41]   See "J.K. Rowling Writes about Her Reasons for Speaking out on Sex and Gender Issues," June 10, 2020, https://www.jkrowling.com/answers/.

[42]   See "A Letter on Justice and Open Debate," *Harper's Magazine*, July 7, 2020, https://harpers.org/a-letter-on-justice-and-open-debate/.

[43]   It should be acknowledged that attempting to silence opposing views is not a new tactic and it has been used by the political left and the political right. Concerning our current sexual politics, however, the practice is generally the tool of self-identified political progressives.

[44]   During the writing of this book, the web seller Amazon.com pulled Ryan Anderson's *When Harry Became Sally* immediately after the "Equality Act" was introduced in the U.S. House of Representatives. The legislation aims to create broad protections in civil

attack on the person who is "canceled" is enabled by technology, particularly social media. Both the aim and the effect of this phenomenon are to curtail speech through intimidation or fear of being the victim of an electronic mob attack. That makes "canceling" contrary to the ideals of a classical understanding of politics and of a liberal democracy such as the United States.[45]

Though more frequently employed by the political left on this issue, cancel culture's attacks embody a form of intellectual fascism. As the barnyard cabals of George Orwell's 1945 novel *Animal Farm* vividly illustrate, the totalitarian impulses of the far-right and the far-left ultimately converge; the extremes of modern politics form not a line but a circle. And, ironically, the distortions of language promoted by gender ideology's enforcement of political correctness recalls another of Orwell's novels—the dystopian classic *1984*.

---

rights law for those identifying as transgender, non-binary, or gay or lesbian by recognizing sexual orientation and gender identity as protected legal classes. See Matt Hadro, "Scholar Ryan Anderson's Critique of Transgender Movement Reportedly De-Listed by Amazon," *National Catholic Register*, February 22, 2021, https://www.ncregister.com/cna/scholar-ryan-andersons-critique-of-transgender-movement-reportedly-de-listed-by-amazon; and Anderson's own take in "When Amazon Erased My Book" in *First Things* (February 23, 2021): https://www.firstthings.com/web-exclusives/2021/02/when-amazon-erased-my-book. It is hard to see this as anything other than a corporation engaging in cancel culture's suppression of speech.

[45] See the thoughtful analysis provided by V. Bradley Lewis, *National Catholic Register*, "Canceled by the Cancel Culture," July 14, 2020, https://www.ncregister.com/daily-news/canceled-by-the-cancel-culture.

The Abolition of Man and Woman

That which is ultimately "canceled" by gender ideology is human nature—the human person as a composite of a sexually differentiated body and a soul. Gender ideology sees the body not as the visible expression of the person—a real manifestation and window into the depth of the personal subject—but as a surface or screen on which to project a self-articulated identity. Personal identity is a construct decided and projected or performed by the individual. The body must be brought into conformity with this identity. In itself, the body has no inherent meaning. Its sexual characteristics can actually inhibit the individual's desires and self-articulation and so can and should be reshaped. The anthropology—or understanding of the human person—that emerges from this perspective is unmistakably dualist. The human person is seen as comprised of mind and will. The body is, therefore, regarded as superfluous to this self or even a hindrance to it. Like many of the dualisms of the ancient world, the body comes to be viewed as a kind of prison from which one needs to escape or, failing this, at least remake.

It is not accidental that the book of Genesis connects the image of God to the duality of "male and female" (Gn 1:27). Sexual difference orients us toward communion with one another. It is among the most basic and irreducible positive features of human diversity, deeper than racial or ethnic differences. If males and females with different racial or ethnic features intermarry, the physical differences between them (e.g., skin color or facial features) will be blended in their children. But they will continue to produce offspring who are themselves male or female. In the sexual union of male and female in the marriage covenant, men and women are able to receive the gift of a new human being also made in the image of God (see Gn 1:28). Procreation is, as Pope St. John Paul II taught, a renewal of the mystery of creation when God brought forth human life on the earth.[46] At the same time, Christian revelation shows that because God Himself is an eternal communion of Persons, our relationality of sexual dimension actually mirrors the Trinitarian mystery.

Unlike Christian theology, which elevates the relational difference between male and female, gender ideology seeks to undermine it—or even eliminate it. For instance, this ideology threatens particular protections for women in public life. Critics of the recent *Bostock* ruling of the Supreme Court were quick to point out that extending Title VII protections of the 1964 Civil Rights Acts to persons who identify as transgender poses a threat to the social and economic gains by women in public life and even to women's safety. Jennifer Roback Morse decried the ruling as the end of womanhood: "The Supreme Court's decision in *Bostock v. Clayton County* erases womanhood. It is the end of women in sports and women's rights to privacy. Thanks to the Sexual Revolutionaries on the Court, our laws will refuse to distinguish men who say they are women from real women."[47] These concerns are not mere distractions. Biological males who identify as transgender—even if they have undergone hormonal

---

[46] See his weekly General Audiences of March 26, 1980, and October 6, 1982.

[47] See "SCOTUS Erases Womanhood," June 16, 2020, http://www.ruthinstitute.org/ruth-speaks-out/ruth-institute-scotus-erases-womanhood.

transitioning—have significant competitive advantages over biological women in athletic competition.[48] Likewise, there are issues of privacy and safety for women forced to share public bathroom or locker room facilities with biological men who identify as transgender—issues that are particularly acute for women who were previously victims of sexual abuse or assault by men.[49] There have also been a number of criminal cases in which male sexual predators have posed as transgender women in order to gain access to women's only spaces in public facilities.[50] Pointing to these very real dangers does not make people like Roback Morse or J.K. Rowling "TERFs"—it makes them realists who are concerned with protecting women's rights and safety.

More broadly still, gender ideology dissolves the very idea of sexual difference. David Crawford and Michael Hanby argue that the *Bostock* ruling effectively abolishes both sexes—not just the female sex. The majority opinion holds that both a man who identifies as a woman and a biological woman are "similarly situated" in regard to the law in order to prohibit sex-based discrimination. This legal language game conceals a deeper philosophical judgment—that personal subjectivity and identity are only arbitrarily related to the body. They note the consequences that follow from this judgment:

---

[48]   See Anderson, *When Harry Became Sally*, 190–92.

[49]   See Ryan Anderson, "A Brave New World of Transgender Policy," *Harvard Journal of Law and Public Policy* 41, no. 1 (2018): 309–54; see esp. 320–27.

[50]   For an overview of safety concerns and a summary of a number of these criminal cases, see Anderson, "Brave New World," 327–35.

It is impossible to redefine human nature for only
one person. When a fourth-grade girl is required to
affirm in thought, word and deed that a boy in her
class is now a girl, this does not simply affirm the class-
mate's right to self-expression. It calls into question the
meaning of "boy" and "girl" as such, thereby also calling into question both her own "identity" and that of
everyone in her life, from her mother and father to her
brothers and sisters, and all of her friends and relatives.
As well it should. If each of us is defined by a "gender identity" only arbitrarily related to our male and
female bodies, now relegated to a meaningless biological substrate, then there is no longer any such thing
as man or woman. We are all transgender now, even if
sex and "gender identity" accidentally coincide in an
overwhelming majority of instances.[51]

As a consequence of this ruling, from the standpoint of
the law, the body and its sexual characteristics do not matter
in determining personal identity. This holds for all people—
not just those who would describe themselves as transgender.
The implementation and enforcement of this ruling across a
society cannot help but be totalitarian in nature.

In the United States, the implementation of this totalitarian impulse at the federal level can be witnessed in the
Equality Act (H.R. 5) that the U.S. House of Representatives passed on February 25, 2021. This legislation, if signed
into law, would federalize many of the aggressive features

---

[51]   See "The Abolition of Man and Woman," *The Wall Street Journal*, June 24, 2020, https://www.wsj.com/articles/the-abolition-of
-man-and-woman-11593017500.

of gender ideology mentioned here: coercing speech; undermining protections for women in public spaces, the workplace, and athletics; jeopardizing religious freedom for groups and institutions; undermining parents' rights to raise their children; and forcing medical professionals to provide transitioning procedures despite medical or conscience-based objections that they might have.[52]

The dissolution of human nature and sexual difference contained in the *Bostock* ruling and Equality Act points to a deeper dissociation of language and reality.

The Babel Effect

The story of the Tower of Babel in Genesis 11 is, in some ways, a replay of the story of the first human sin in Genesis 3 but on a social scale. Despite the chaos recounted in the previous chapters, the opening of the chapter sounds an idyllic note: "The whole world had the same language and the same words" (Gn 11:1). Once again, humanity's self-reliance led to its undoing. However, instead of overreaching at the instigation of the serpent who promised the human couple that the fruit would make them "like gods, who know good and evil" (Gn 3:5), this time the instigation to pride seems to come from within: "Let us build ourselves a city and a tower with its top in the sky" (Gn 11:4). The implication is that this tower would put human beings on an equal footing with God.

---

[52]   See the analysis provided by the USCCB, "Truth about the Equality Act," available at https://www.usccb.org/equality-act#tab--back grounders.

A number of the story's features associate the place of this ill-conceived construction project with Babylon, the superpower of six-century B.C. that destroyed Jerusalem and its Temple and deported much of the population of Judah. The people settle in "the land of Shinar" (Gn 11:2)—another name for the area of ancient Babylon. The Hebrew phrase describing the structure, *ūmiḡdāl wərōšōw ḥaššāmayim* ("tower with its top in the sky"), recalls the chief temple of Babylon's warrior god Marduk. The temple's name was *Esaila* (which means "the house that raises high its head"). This temple sat on a ziggurat, which was a tower made of receding stories. The name that the place is given after God's intervention—Babel (see Gn 11:9) was the Hebrew name for Babylon. This name itself contains a note of derision because, whereas the Babylonians understood the name of their city (*Babili*) to indicate "the gate of god," it sounds like the Hebrew *balal* ("he confused"). In short, it is clear that the Babel story is associated with Babylon, and so the great city and powerful nation symbolize human confusion and the failure of human overreach.

The story is a cautionary tale about how human pride and trying to usurp the place of God can lead to disaster on a global scale. Even the most powerful of nations are not immune, and their status makes them particularly susceptible to human pride. As in Genesis 3, the effects of sin are division of human beings from one another and from God. In this case, however, there are additional effects. The people are scattered "over all the earth" (Gn 11:8), and their language is confused.

It is worth pondering this story in light of our contemporary multiplication of genders and Pope Benedict's words about the loss of an understanding of ourselves as creatures quoted in the previous chapter. Recall Pope Benedict's words: "Man calls his nature into question. . . . Man and woman in their created state as complementary versions of what it means to be human are disputed."[53] When we lose an awareness of ourselves as the creatures who are the beloved handiwork of a loving Creator, we are easily overcome by the kind of Promethean hubris that we see in the peoples of the world described in the story of Babel. We deny our own human nature and its limitations. We reach for the heavens to remake ourselves and, in so doing, are plunged deeper into confusion and alienation from our Creator and our fellow human beings. Sadly, the signs of gender ideology are evident throughout our present, confused world: the use of educational programs to indoctrinate children, the ideological colonization of law, the reconfiguration of family, and the misdirection of medicine away from its historic aims and ethical basis.

I want to focus on and underscore, however, one further effect here—the disconnection of language from reality as opposed to an interrelation between the two. Philosophers speak of two basic ways of understanding our use of language with the world around us—realism and nominalism. The realist position holds that like things (things of a common kind) have a nature or essence that unites them within that group of things. For example, individual trees have a certain

---

[53]   Benedict XVI, "Christmas Address to the Roman Curia" (December 21, 2012).

nature or essence that corresponds with that of other trees and is what makes the individual tree a tree. The same is so with human beings. The realist further holds that our use of language maps onto this reality—when we use a universal concept like "tree" or "human being," it corresponds to the actual natures or essence in the tree or human being. Nominalists, on the other hand, hold that there are not common natures or essences in things and, thus, universal concepts do not correspond to actual natures of things. For moderate nominalists (also called conceptualists), these universal concepts exist only in the human mind as a way of organizing things that appear to be similar. Thus, "tree" is an organizing construct that exists only in the human mind. For more radical nominalists, reality is utterly individual—there are no unifying patterns in reality, whether in being or in language. The correspondence between language and reality, then, is ultimately arbitrary. In this view, the word "tree" has no real correspondence to anything in the world around us or even in our minds.

The rejection of our own status as creatures rooted in a sexually differentiated body designed by our Creator unmoors us from both the reality of our own identity and the way that language can faithfully capture reality as a whole. Our society is increasingly adopting a radical nominalist view of gender and, therefore, words like "gender," "male," or "female" have no real connection to the world around us. The result is the proliferation of genders, words to describe them, and pronouns to capture a growing multitude of self-articulated identities. Our post-Babel spread of genders is a symptom of a fundamental loss of confidence in the truthfulness of words to convey a reality that we did not create. Gender ideology rejects both the realist's belief in a reality where things have common natures or essences and in the ability of language to correspond with that reality. Like Humpty-Dumpty, we seek to make ourselves masters in the "Looking-Glass World" by bending words to our own personal act of the will. But, as the story of Babel reminds us, any attempt to make ourselves like God will lead only to disarray. And this disarray cannot be reversed by an individual will to power—even multiplied many times over across a culture. It takes Pentecost—the sending of the Holy Spirit who bears witness to the truth of the gospel message—to begin to overcome the fragmentation and alienation unleashed by human hubris and sin.[54]

The next chapter will continue unpacking Pope Benedict's insights on how we have strayed from our identity by looking at the disconnect between gender and sex caused by modern philosophy and second-wave feminism.

---

[54] Luke's account of Pentecost in Acts 2 is in many ways a mirror image of the disaster of Babel in Genesis 11. It is for this reason that the Church includes Genesis 11:1–9 as an option for the First Reading for the Vigil of Pentecost.

CHAPTER THREE

ENGENDERING DISCUSSION: THE PHILOSOPHICAL ROOTS

Two evils my people have done: they have forsaken me,
the source of living waters; They have dug themselves cis-
terns, broken cisterns that cannot hold water.

—Jeremiah 2:13

The end goal of feminist revolution must be . . . not just the elim-
ination of male privilege but of the sex distinction itself: genital
differences between human beings would no longer matter culturally.
—Shulamith Firestone, *The Dialectic of Sex:*
The Case for Feminist Revolution

If the immutable character of sex is contested, perhaps this construct
called "sex" is as culturally constructed as gender; indeed, perhaps it
was always already gender, with the consequence that the distinc-
tion between sex and gender turns out to be no distinction at all.
—Judith Butler, *Gender Trouble:*
Feminism and the Subversion of Identity

Some thirty years ago, we were seated around the dining room table for a family lunch. At that point, we had three children who were six years, three years, and about six months of age. Our three-year-old daughter, Bekah, surveyed the room and decided (as three-year-olds do) to identify everyone in the room by their gender. "Daddy's a boy, Mommy's a girl, Rachel's a girl, Paul's a boy," she pronounced. Her big sister Rachel decided to give the conversation a theological turn and interrogate her younger sister at the same time, "What about Jesus?" The three-year-old responded, "Jesus is Jesus." Her six-year-old sister corrected her, "No, Jesus is a boy." The three-year-old was undaunted, "Jesus is Jesus." Her older sister repeated in exasperation, "No, Jesus is a boy." As I later told my students, having just finished my dissertation on sexual difference, I was amazed to find what sounded like proto-feminist theology around our family lunch table.

As with the term gender, which was discussed in the previous chapter, feminism too, not long ago, had a very different meaning. What historians often refer to as the "first wave" of feminism, which emerged in the eighteenth and nineteenth centuries and crested in the early twentieth century, had a mixed pedigree but a largely positive focus. It drew from the human rights language of the Enlightenment, from socialist thought and politics, and from Evangelical Christianity. The involvement of American and British women in the revivalist movements gave birth to women's public activism, eventually leading to their efforts to abolish slavery and the promotion of public purity campaigns and the temperance movement. But these female activist's efforts to effect social and political change was frustrated because they lacked the right to vote, which allowed male politicians to not take them seriously. The movement thus coalesced in the push for women's suffrage, and much of its momentum dissipated when this was granted by many western countries in the early twentieth century.[1] Less well known is the fact that most "first wave" feminists were staunchly pro-life, pro-mother-hood, and pro-sexual difference. As Erika Bachiochi notes: "America's pioneering feminists, such as Susan B. Anthony and Elizabeth Cady Stanton, fought for the right to vote and for fair treatment in the workplace. American's pioneering feminists uniformly opposed abortion, because they saw it as an attack on women *as women*, those uniquely endowed with the ability to bear children."[2]

If feminism once had such noble aspirations and convictions concerning the human condition, especially the unique gifts of women and the goodness of sexual difference, then why the change? The story is complex. Parts of it will be sketched in this chapter and in the next.

The Dissolution of Nature, Being, and Sex

Pope Benedict XVI traces the origins of gender ideology to the work of Simon de Beauvoir. Beauvoir was a colleague, collaborator, and lover of the twentieth-century existentialist philosopher Jean Paul Sartre and served to refine and disseminate his work, along with bringing it into a feminist context in her own writing.

---

[1]   For a relatively "non-partisan" history of the first and second "waves" of feminism covered here, see *Olive Banks, Faces of Feminism: A Study of Feminism as a Social Movement* (New York: St. Martin's, 1981).
[2]   "The Uniqueness of Woman: Church Teaching on Abortion" in *Women, Sex and the Church: A Case for Catholic Teaching*, Erika Bachiochi, ed. (Boston: Pauline, 2010), 41 (emphasis in original).

For Sartre, "existence precedes essence."[3] Contrary to philosophers like Aristotle, there is no human nature that a person actualizes and that is the basis of his or her flourishing. It is up to us to fashion our own identity and our self-definition with existence in order to answer the question of what it means to be human. But this is something that is ultimately impossible because human existence is open-ended, a question that refuses an answer. In any event, the ultimate basis of Sartre's claim is theological: "There is no human nature, since there is no God to conceive it."[4] The universe is devoid of a loving Creator and, thus, devoid of meaning. Human existence is, therefore, characterized by absurdity and a kind of hopelessness because there is no overall telos or end for human freedom. One can strive for authenticity—being true to oneself, however understood—but there no ultimate point or fulfillment to be found in doing so. It is little wonder that Catholic thinkers like Josef Pieper used Sartre as a dialogue partner since he offers a consistent atheistic philosophy based on the rejection of the theology of creation.[5]

---

[3] This phrase, which many see as a key to Sartre's thought as a whole, was first made in a lecture given in 1945. It was published the following year as *Existentialism is a Humanism*, trans. Carol Macomber, preface by Arlene Elkaïm-Sartre, ed. John Kulka (New Haven: Yale, 2007), vii.

[4] Jean-Paul Sartre, *Existentialism and Human Emotions* (New York: Philosophical Library, 1957), 15. Similarly, she writes: "We remind man that there is no law-maker other than himself, and that in his forlornness he will decide by himself" (ibid. 50, 51).

[5] See, for example, Pieper's "Creatureliness and Human Nature" in *For the Love of Wisdom: Essays on the Nature of Philosophy*, ed. Berthold Wald, trans. Roger Wasserman (San Francisco: Ignatius Press, 2006).

Beauvoir carried this same philosophical outlook into a feminist context in her book *The Second Sex*. She assigns women this name because of what she sees as their perennial status as "other" and "afterthought" in classical thought—woman is defined by her lack of male (and, hence, human) qualities for Aristotle and is an "imperfect" or "incidental" being for St. Thomas Aquinas.[6] For Beauvoir, this perceived otherness has been the basis of women's subjugation and oppression by men throughout history. The existentialist axiom that existence precedes essence is now recast in the sharp distinction between gender and sex flagged by Pope Benedict XVI: "One is not born but becomes a woman."[7] The social construction of gender also points the way to women's liberation from oppression. As a construct, gender norms can be cast off or reconstituted in more egalitarian terms. They have no basis in biology or in human nature—the former is raw material for human freedom, and the latter simply does not exist.

These existentialist assumptions left a deep imprint on the intellectual articulation of second wave feminism that took shape in the women's liberation movement of the 1960s and 70s, even making their way into the emerging field of feminist theology. Many feminist thinkers saw sex as largely the work of socialization and culture. For these "constructionist" thinkers, sex and gender are distinct realities. Sex refers to the anatomical and biological differences between males and females. Gender is the socially constructed *meaning* of

---

6   See Simon de Beauvoir, *The Second Sex*, trans. H. M. Parshley (London: Jonathan Cape, 1953), Introduction.

7   Beauvoir, *The Second Sex*, 267.

these differences concerning roles or attributes commonly assigned to one sex or the other.

Because these thinkers wished to emphasize and advocate for social and political equality between women and men, they often downplayed difference and emphasized the sameness or even interchangeability of the sexes. Everything beyond the biological difference necessary for sexual reproduction was, therefore, relegated to the sphere of "gender"—a social construct created to support the subordination of women to men. Thus, Catholic feminist theologian Rosemary Radford Ruether could write, "Maleness and femaleness exist as reproductive role specialization. There is no necessary (biological) connection between reproductive complementarity in either psychological or social role differentiation. These are the works of culture and socialization, not of 'nature.'"[8]

As noted above, however, at the heart of modern existentialism is the rejection of the theology of creation and the corresponding idea of a human nature that is the basis of a person's flourishing and identity. One no longer actualizes what he or she is as human, but one becomes what one chooses. This explains the openness of many feminist thinkers to various forms of process and postmodern thought.

Having some roots in nineteenth-century German idealism, process thought was first fully articulated in the work of twentieth-century British mathematician turned philosopher Alfred North Whitehead. Drawing heavily on the evolutionary view of the world produced by the work of Charles

---

[8]   Rosemary Radford Ruether, *Sexism & God Talk: Toward a Feminist Theology* (Boston: Beacon, 1983), 228.

Darwin, Whitehead rejected classical conceptions of not only nature but also being itself. Everything instead is understood as process—as becoming. This includes not just the material world but God as well. God is therefore collapsed into creation in a form of pantheism.[9] In the hands of feminist theologians like Ruether, this process view dissolves the distinction between God and creation within an ecologically interdependent universe in which the "God/dess" progressively realizes itself. Her "ecofeminism" also results in the denial of the Christian ideas of the immortality of the soul and the resurrection of the body. The individual bundles of energy of deceased human beings are simply absorbed into the collective personhood of God/dess that serves as a cosmic memory of the human beings having existed. As human bodies decay into the earth, "our existence ceases as an individual ego/organism and dissolves back into the cosmic matrix of matter/energy, from which new centers of individuation arise."[10] Such an overtly pagan theology bears little resemblance to the core concepts of Christian faith.

This rejection of the classical conceptions of God and creation paved the way for the more complete dissolution of an understanding of being in the postmodern turn embraced by many subsequent feminist scholars. Postmodern thought reacts not only against traditional concepts of classical philosophy, such as nature or being, but also against more modern (Enlightenment) claims that ground truth in a universal rationality or a scientific account of reality. Postmodern

---

[9]   In this way, process thought empties the universe of God as understood with Christian tradition and classical philosophy.

[10]   Ruether, *Sexism & God Talk*, 257; see also 256–58.

thinkers reject these "foundationalist" claims, arguing that these accounts of reason or science are constructs that ultimately mask relations of power. Logic, reason, and truth themselves are called into question and ultimately seen as constructs or assertions of groups in power. There are no universal truths or objective moral values, and claims to the contrary can themselves be deconstructed.

Concerning sexual difference, not only human nature but also the gender binary itself can, therefore, be deconstructed. For feminist postmodern philosopher Judith Butler, not only is "gender" a construct but so is "sex"—the individual within specific cultural contexts performs both. Thus, she writes, "Perhaps this construct called 'sex' is as culturally constructed as gender; indeed, perhaps it was always already gender with the consequence that the distinction between sex and gender turns out to be no distinction at all."[11] The body and sex are both "produced" by the individual in specific power relations:

> The body is not "sexed" in any significant sense prior to its determination within a discourse through which it becomes invested with an "idea" of natural or essential sex. The body gains meaning within discourse only in the context of power relations. Sexuality is an historically specific organization of power, of discourse, of bodies and of affectivity. As such, sexuality is understood by Foucault to produce "sex" as an artificial

---

[11]   Judith Butler, *Gender Trouble: Feminism and the Subversion of Identity*, Routledge Classics, 36 (New York: Routledge, 1990), 9.

concept which effectively extends and disguises the power relations responsible for its genesis."[12]

Here, we have a philosophical basis for the fluidity of bodily identity and the proliferation of genders described in the last chapter. There is no givenness in the body, gender, or sex. These can mean whatever the individual chooses for them within his or her own consciousness and social context—whatever he or she performs as a self or "writes" as a gender identity. The sexually differentiated person is now collapsed into the pre-Christian *persona*—a mask or the role in a performance.[13]

It is a fascinating "sign of the times" to witness the growing disconnect mentioned in the last chapter between more standard second wave feminists still pursuing an egalitarian vision of gender justice and those in subsequent waves influenced by postmodern thought and queer theory, with the former worrying about the impact of things like biological males who identify as females competing in women's athletics and the latter dismissing such concerns as "transphobic." Having sown the existentialist and postmodern wind, modern feminism now faces a transgender whirlwind to which it helped to give birth.

---

[12]   Butler, *Gender Trouble*, 92.
[13]   Historical study has shown that the concept of person as we know it actually emerged from the early Church's reflection on the mysteries of Christ and the Trinity. See, for example, the masterful treatment in Joseph Ratzinger, *Introduction to Christianity*, trans. J.R. Foster and Michael J. Miller (San Francisco: Ignatius Press, 2004), 178–90.

A Marxist Vision of Gender Liberation

Beauvoir's deployment of existentialist philosophy was not merely intended to be diagnostic—it was meant to identify the sources of women's oppression in order to enable their liberation. Both she and Sartre drew freely from Karl Marx's works, whose thought and politics they saw as a resource for bettering the human condition.

Marx shares many affinities with some of the modern philosophical currents just sampled. Like existentialism, Marxism articulates an atheistic view of the universe that dismisses concepts found in Scripture and classical philosophy such as nature or being. Like postmodern thought, it eschews the idea of truth or universal moral values and focuses on the power relations from which such concepts emerge. Like process thought, it has roots in the idealist philosophy of G.W.F. Hegel but sees the unfolding of history in materialist and economic rather than idealist terms. It is not surprising that existentialist or postmodern thinkers are often implicitly or explicitly Marxist in their politics. Marxist social analysis and focus on praxis (i.e., practical action) are seen as important tools for effecting change within specific cultures.

Second wave feminism was greatly influenced by the Marxist view of marriage and the family and even sexual difference as vehicles of oppression for women. In their 1848 *Communist Manifesto,* Marx and his collaborator, Fredrich Engels, call for the abolition of the family:

> Abolition [*Aufhebung*] of the family! Even the most radical flare up at this infamous proposal of the Communists. . . . On what foundation is the present family,

the bourgeois family, based? On capital, on private
gain. In its completely developed form, this family
exists only among the bourgeoisie. But this state of
things finds its complement in the practical absence
of the family among the proletarians, and in public
prostitution.[14]

From this perspective, the family is an agent of capital-
ism and serves to maintain the hierarchical status of the
bourgeoise (or ruling classes). Once this system and class
are overthrown, the family will disappear along with it. In
this oppressive system, "the bourgeois sees his wife as a mere
instrument of production."[15] Sexual fidelity or monogamy
is an illusion because of the existence of prostitution and
widespread adultery among the ruling classes. It follows that
working to undermine or overthrow the family is a way to
hasten an oppressive capitalist system's defeat. In his 1884
book *The Origin of the Family* (published a year after Marx's
death but written with his input), Engels outlined a plan
for putting this strategy into action, calling for an end to
monogamous marriage, the promotion of extramarital sex
for unmarried women, ending religious education, putting
women to work in factories, moving children into daycare
facilities, and having the state replace parents in raising and
educating children.

This program sounds very much like the playbook followed
by the proponents, not just of Soviet-style communism, but

---

[14]   Karl Marx and Frederick Engels, *The Communist Manifesto*, trans.
        Samuel Moore, vol. 6 of Karl Marx and Frederick Engels, Collect-
        ed Works (London, 1976; rpt. London: ElecBook, 1998), p. 32.
[15]   Ibid., p. 33.

also of the architects and evangelists of the Sexual Revolution in the West. The aims and impact of that cultural shift will be considered more fully in the next chapter, but here it is worth noting Marxism's impact on second wave feminism. Many of its leaders and thinkers were influenced by Marxist ideas, either from contact with Marx's own work, or through its intellectual dissemination by groups like the Frankfurt School.

Others have pointed out that, at least in its beginnings, second wave feminism shared a fair amount of continuity with the aims and ideals of the first wave. But, while that movement coalesced with a focus on achieving a political voice for women and so dissipated with women's suffrage in many western countries in the early twentieth century, the movement that began in the 1960s initially set its sights on greater economic equality for women. The Sexual Revolution, which was hitting high gear with the development of oral contraception, was a separate entity. As Sue Ellen Browder puts it in her book *Subverted*: "In the beginning the women's movement and the sexual revolution were *distinctly separate* cultural phenomena."[16] The book goes on to chronicle, from a first-person perspective, how this changed. The leaders of the women's liberation movement became convinced that the key to achieving economic and social equality with men could only be accomplished by suppressing women's distinctive fertility via large-scale contraception and abortion. Women could be equal to men only if they were freed from the shackles of their fertility, from

---

[16]   Sue Ellen Browder, *Subverted: How I Helped the Sexual Revolution Hijack the Women's Movement* (San Francisco: Ignatius, 2019), 11; (emphasis in original).

pregnancy, from childbirth, and from marriage that bound them. This represents a 180-degree turn from the position held by most of the first wave feminist pioneers. Marx and Engel's plan for liberation from the institution of the family clearly shaped these feminist leaders. [17]

Marxist's ideas saturated the literature of the Sexual Revolution. An example of a full-scale feminist vision of women's liberation is evident in Shulamith Firestone's influential 1970 book *The Dialectic of Sex*. Firestone's analysis of women's oppression and the path to overcoming it draws on the action plan put forward by Marx and Engels but uses technology to go beyond it:

> Just as to ensure elimination of economic classes requires the revolt of the underclass (the proletariat) and, in a temporary dictatorship, their seizure of the means of production, so to assure the elimination of sexual classes requires the revolt of the underclass (women) and the seizure of control of reproduction: not only the full restoration to women of ownership of their own bodies, but also their seizure of control of human fertility—the new population biology as well as all the social institutions of child-bearing and child-rearing. . . . The end goal of feminist revolution

---

[17]   On the influence of Marxist ideas on some of the leaders of the feminist movement of the 60s and 70s see Carrie Gress, *The Anti-Mary Exposed: Rescuing the Culture from Toxic Femininity* (Charlotte, NC: TAN Books, 2019), esp. chapters five and six. See also the wider treatment of the impact of Marxism on the family in the West offered by Paul Kengor in *Takedown: From Communists to Progressives, How the Left Has Sabotaged Family and Marriage* (Washington, DC: WND Books, 2015).

must be, unlike that of the first feminist movement, not just the elimination of male privilege but of the sex distinction itself: genital differences between human beings would no longer matter culturally.[18]

Marx's analysis of oppressive structures is no longer here confined to class but is extended to sex as the cause of women's oppression at the hands of a patriarchal society. Contraception, abortion, and emerging forms of laboratory reproduction held the keys to their liberation. Firestone's revolutionary program called for replacing pregnancy with gestating children in artificial wombs so that women would be on an equal footing with men and abolishing the nuclear family by collectivized child rearing.[19] The result would be the abolition of any significance given to sexual difference at least concerning social and political praxis. The presupposition of this Marxist feminist program is clear—sexual difference itself is unjust and must be overcome as much as possible.

While the influence of Marxism has receded from many parts of the world, its influence in the West appears to be on the rise. It is not so much, however, its analysis of economic estrangement but of other forms of alienation due to differences of race, sex, or gender that have seemingly captured many people's minds and imaginations, giving birth to what some describe as a "woke" culture of political activism.

---

18   Shulamith Firestone, *The Dialectic of Sex: The Case for Feminist Revolution* (New York: William Morrow, 1970), 221; see also p. 11.
19   See ibid., 25.

Broken Cisterns, Poisoned Wells

Why travel so far down the rabbit hole in pursuing some of the intellectual sources of gender ideology? One reason is that we are, thereby, following the path indicated by Pope Benedict XVI in his diagnosis of the origin of this phenomenon. Another is that these intellectual streams still flow through our culture and through gender ideology, shaping the way people see themselves and the world around them. They continue to influence the way many people think about the body, sexual difference, and marriage. Tracing them to their source helps us to better understand why these waters are bitter and why they fail to satisfy those who drink from them.

In the sixth century B.C., as part of a covenant lawsuit (*rîb*) brought by the prophet on behalf of God, Jeremiah indicted his countrymen in Judah for a twofold sin: forsaking God who alone is "the source of living waters" and digging for themselves "broken cisterns that cannot hold water" (Jer 2:13). Jeremiah here refers to the people's abandonment of their covenant with the one true God for the worship of idols. Only God can offer the "living waters" of life and peace to His people. The people's efforts to find security in alliances with other nations and their gods (see 2:18) are futile, like trying to use "broken cisterns" to collect rainwater. The result will be disastrous (see 2:15)—the suffering of conquest and exile.

This bleak picture is replicated in our own cultural situation. Gender ideology clearly rejects our status as creatures and co-creators with God since our nature includes sexually differentiated bodies capable of transmitting life through the union of man and woman in the covenant of marriage. Having cast off this reality as false and oppressive, this ideology seeks alternate explanations based entirely on secular currents of modern thought. In a universe empty of an infinitely powerful and loving God, gender ideology fashions its answers to what it means to be human without reference to categories such as nature, being, or truth. There are no transcendent moral values—only a struggle for justice conceived as sameness to be pursued through revolutionary means. The body, sex, and marriage must be rethought and reconfigured insofar as they further the oppression of individuals or groups. Yet, these musings of modernity's various atheistic humanisms are nothing more than our contemporary "broken cisterns," incapable of containing the waters of life-giving truth.

In the fourth chapter of John's Gospel, we find again a reference to "living water" (v. 10). This time it is offered by Jesus to a woman of Samaria—an individual regarded as ritually impure by the Jewish leaders of Jesus' day due to her status as a woman and a person regarded as tainted by impure blood and worship. Further, she is a person who has been profoundly wounded in her sexual relationships—having had five husbands and now living with a man outside of marriage (see Jn 4:18). As often happens in John's Gospel, she misunderstands Jesus' words and the meaning of His offer thinking that He meant "flowing water" versus the still water contained within Jacob's well. She takes His words as pertaining to physical life (*bios*) rather than the fullness of life (*zóé*) that Jesus, the new and greater Jacob, offers her.[20] This water is that of the Holy Spirit made available through the

---

[20]   See Benedict XVI, *Jesus of Nazareth: From the Baptism in the Jordan to the Transfiguration*, trans. Adrian Walker (New York: Image, 2007), 240–41.

rending of Jesus' body (the new and greater Temple) on the Cross. In His being "lifted up" on the Cross (see Jn 12:32), Jesus is the New Adam in whom humanity is recreated:

> The open side of the new Adam repeats the mystery of the "open side" of man at creation: it is the beginning of a new definitive community of men with one another, a community symbolized here by blood and water, in which John points to the basic Christian sacraments of baptism and Eucharist, and through them to the Church as the sign of the new community of men.[21]

The Samaritan woman of John 4 represents a type of our culture and the many people dwelling within it who are affected by the growing gender confusion. Our efforts to create an identity and happiness apart from the One who created us and the world in which we live only leaves us empty and isolated. Yet, our philosophical categories to articulate this self-definition are "broken cisterns" that hold no water or at best offer a water that is not life-giving. Defining what it means to be human, performing an identity, or pursuing this worldly liberation through justice understood as sameness are profoundly different than recognizing our existence, our bodies, and our sexual differences as gifts from God and as integral to His plan for us. Like the woman at the well, we need to encounter the One who offers us the healing of life and truth—the One who alone is the source of the "living water" for which we thirst.

---

[21]   Ratzinger, *Introduction to Christianity*, 241; see also Benedict XVI, *Jesus of Nazareth*, 242–43.

CHAPTER FOUR

THREE REVOLUTIONS

"Is there beauty in Sodom? Believe me, that for the immense mass of mankind beauty is found in Sodom. Did you know that secret? The awful thing is that beauty is mysterious as well as terrible. God and the devil are fighting there and the battlefield is the heart of man."
—Fyodor Dostoevsky, *The Brothers Karamazov*

You say you want a revolution; Well, you know; We all want to change the world.
—The Beatles, "Revolution"

I'll tip my hat to the new constitution; Take a bow for the new revolution; Smile and grin at the change all around; Pick up my guitar and play; Just like yesterday; Then I'll get on my knees and pray; We don't get fooled again.
—The Who, "Won't Get Fooled Again"

Then I saw a new heaven and a new earth. The former heaven and the former earth had passed away, and the sea was no more. I also saw the holy city, a new Jerusalem, coming down out of heaven from God, prepared as a bride adorned for her husband.
—Revelation 21:1–2

Scripture begins and ends with a wedding. In Genesis 2, the man (*'āḏām*) binds himself to the woman whom God created for him in the covenant of marriage. His covenant declaration is recorded in verse 23: "This one, at last, is bone of my bones and flesh of my flesh; This one shall be called woman, for out of man this one has been taken." The language of "bone and flesh" is used elsewhere in Scripture to denote covenant allegiance, covering the possibilities of power or strength (symbolized by the reference to "bone") and weakness (symbolized by the language of "flesh").[1] But the covenant between this first human pair is possible because they are woman (*'iššāh*) and man (*îš*).[2] It is only as such that they can receive the blessing of fertility by which they exercise dominion within creation as made in the image of God (see Gn 1:28).

In Revelation 21, we are presented with a vision of the final transformation of the world at the end of time. The "new heaven and new earth" that God creates again are described in nuptial terms. The elimination of the sea represents the final overcoming of the forces of chaos and evil begun in the act of God creating all things by His Word (see Gn 2:2). As in the Old Testament, the city of Jerusalem is used to symbolize God's covenant people. This, however, is the "new Jerusalem," the gathering of all the redeemed of the nations. It is this redeemed people who are adorned as a bride, identifying them with the bride of the victorious

---

[1] See the covenant declarations of the tribes of the northern kingdom to David when they pledged their allegiance to him as king in Hebron in 2 Sm 5:1; see also Jgs 9:2; 2 Sm 19:13–14; 1 Chr 11:1.

[2] As will be discussed further in chapter six, the word *'ādām* in Hebrew means "man" in the more generic sense of "the human" or "mankind." The word *îš* is more gender specific and must be understood in reference to its counterpart *'iššāh*.

Lamb mentioned elsewhere in the book (see Rv 21:9; see also 19:7–9; 22:17). Again, as in the Old Testament, marriage is used as a symbol of restoration (see Is 54:1; 62:1–7; Zep 3:14–18). Nevertheless, here it is not just a restoration of the people of Israel to their land after the Babylonian exile. Though the city of Jerusalem and its Temple are again in ruins as of the writing of the book of Revelation, it is not just the people of Israel but also people "from every nation, race, people, and tongue" (Rv 7:9) who form the great multitude of the redeemed before God's throne. The scattering and division caused by human sin begun in the Garden and continued at Babel will finally be overcome through the blood of the Lamb.

This bookending of Scripture with weddings serves to concretize the importance of marriage in God's plan for humanity and for the Church. But we have other testimony—less weighty but more recent—supporting this importance. Father Carlo Caffarra, the Italian priest who served as the founding president of the Pontifical John Paul II Institute for Studies on Marriage and the Family, wrote to Sr. Lucia (one of the Fatima visionaries) in 1984 asking for her prayers for the fledgling institute. He was surprised to receive a reply from the nun in response to his request. In her response, Sr. Lucia wrote:

> "Father, a time will come when the decisive battle between the kingdom of Christ and Satan will be over marriage and the family. . . . And those who will work for the good of the family will experience persecution

and tribulation. But do not be afraid, because Our Lady has already crushed his head."[3]

While taken from a private revelation (though one approved by the Church), Sr. Lucia's ominous yet ultimately hopeful words indicate that Satan, too, knows the importance of marriage and the family in God's plan of salvation for the world and, therefore, seeks to destroy it.

Even though the attack on the civilization of love begins and ends with marriage and the family, as Sr. Lucia's warning makes clear, this strategic attack has taken on many forms besides the intellectual currents discussed in the previous chapter. Unfortunately, there are other attacks that are antithetical to a Judeo-Christian vision of marriage and sexual difference that have been further enabled and empowered by dramatic historical and cultural changes over the last two centuries. Key among these are the three revolutions that have destabilized our understanding of the human person, sexual difference, and the family: the Industrial Revolution, the Sexual Revolution, and the Technological Revolution. The Church's teaching over the last two centuries has been significantly shaped by her response to these challenges.[4]

---

3   Fr. Linus Clovis, "The Final Battle between Our Lord and the Reign of Satan Will Be over Marriage and the Family," Voice of the Family, April 22, 2020, https://voiceofthefamily.com/the-final-battle-between-our-lord-and-the-reign-of-satan-will-be-over-marriage-and-the-family/.

4   Msgr. Brian Bransfield argues that the anthropology of Pope St. John Paul II was developed specifically as a response to these challenges. See Brian Bransfield, *The Human Person: According to John Paul II* (Boston: Pauline, 2009).

The Industrial Revolution

The term Industrial Revolution refers to the transformation of manufacturing processes, especially for textiles, in Europe and the United States between approximately 1760 and 1840, moving from hand production to machines and increasingly using water and steam power. Some scholars and historians speak of a second Industrial Revolution beginning in the later nineteenth century involving the manufacture of steel and the new industries that it enabled. Industrialization is still ongoing in parts of the developing world.

This revolution continues to be a mixed blessing. On the one hand, it made a huge array of goods widely available to working and middle-class people that had previously only been available to the wealthy. On the other hand, it was destructive to the environment on an enormous scale, fouling air, destroying forests, and turning water toxic. It is little wonder that in Tolkien's mythology the imagery he uses to envision the powers of evil are drawn directly from the devastating impact of industrialization on his own beloved English countryside. Describing Saruman, a wizard who has been seduced by evil and who has been destroying an ancient forest to industrialize his fortress of Isengard, Treebeard the Ent says to the hobbits Merry and Pippin: "He is plotting to become a Power. He has a mind of metal and wheels; and he does not care for growing things, except as far as they serve him for the moment."[5] Strongholds of evil in Tolkien's world (such as Saruman's Isengard or Sauron's Mordor) are

---

[5]   J.R.R. Tolkien, *The Two Towers* (New York: Ballantine, 1965), 96.

shrouded in smoke and befouled by ash—the scars of forced industrialization on the natural world.

Even more devastating than the poisoning of the earth and sky was the destruction that the Industrial Revolution sowed within families. As numerous factories sprang up in towns and cities, the working classes were drawn to these industrial centers. Sadly, these people found themselves laboring for long hours for meager pay in often dangerous conditions. This had multiple effects. In families where the father was the principal person to work outside of the home, this removed him from the family and limited his ability to work with his wife in forming their children. Randall Smith describes the problem well:

> It's important to understand that the first fatal blow to the family came during the Industrial Revolution when fathers left the house for the bulk of the day. The deleterious results that followed from ripping fathers away from their children were seen almost immediately in the slums and ghettos of the large industrial towns, as young men, without older men to guide them into adulthood, roamed the streets, un-mentored and un-apprenticed. There, as soon as their hormonal instincts were no longer directed into work or caring for families, they turned to theft and sexual license.[6]

In many poor families, the wages men brought home were not enough to sustain them, so women and children were

---

6   Randall Smith, "A Traditional Catholic Wife?" The Catholic Thing, June 1, 2016, https://www.thecatholicthing.org/2016/06/01/a-traditional-catholic-wife/.

increasingly driven into the workforce with similar long hours, perilous working conditions, and even lower pay. The working poor's plight was devastating to family life—the home simply became a place to sleep and eat.

Yet, the Industrial Revolution had a larger impact on the family in general and not just on those of the working classes. In transforming the home, it also transformed the way in which people thought about children. Prior to this shift, the home for most families was a center of economic activity, as work was often done on the family farm or within the walls of the family house in some form of family business (sometimes called "cottage industries"). The Industrial Revolution largely outsourced work from the home, dividing domestic life from economic productivity. This separation helped to alter the very understanding of children. Since work happened outside of the home, children no longer contributed directly to a family's economic well-being as they did when work was done in the home or on a family farm. Within the space of a few generations, the view of children held by many people flipped from the biblical view of them as a blessing to one that saw them as a burden and a net drain on the family's economic well-being.[7]

The fears about children's negative impact were given pseudo-scientific dressing and extended to the world as a whole in the century that followed. Economic theorist T.R. Malthus's 1798 work *An Essay on the Principle of Population* identified population growth as an ongoing cause of the

---

[7]   See David McCarthy, "Procreation, the Development of Peoples, and the Final Destiny of Humanity," *Communio* 26 (Winter 1999), 698–721.

poverty of the lower classes and a threat that could outstrip large-scale food production. Such growth could be curbed by positive checks (i.e., things that raise the death rate such as war, famine, and natural disaster) and preventative (i.e., contraceptive) means. Such fears were given a particularly shrill articulation in the midst of the twentieth-century expansion of the Sexual Revolution by Paul Erlich's book *The Population Bomb* that predicted widespread famine due to overpopulation in the coming decades.[8] The fact that such apocalyptic scenarios have failed to materialize have done little to dampen the enthusiasm for population control measures in Communist China on the one hand and the wealthy western world on the other.[9]

The Sexual Revolution

The Industrial Revolution's view of children as obstacles to work and economic gain helped fuel the burgeoning Sexual Revolution through the search for more effective contraceptive technologies. The Sexual Revolution was not a wholly twentieth-century phenomenon; these shifting sexual mores

---

[8]   See Paul Erlich, *The Population Bomb* (New York: Ballantine Books, 1968).

[9]   For an overview and critique of population control effects in different parts of the world in the twentieth and twenty-first centuries, see Steven Mosher, *Population Control: Real Costs, Illusory Benefits* (New York: Routledge, 2008). Due to an impending demographic winter, an aging population, and economic hardship in 2015, China modified its coercive "one child policy" to a similarly coercive two-child version. See Lily Kuo and Xueying Wang, "Can China recover from its disastrous one-child policy?" *The Guardian*, March 2, 2019, https://www.theguardian.com/wo rld/2019/mar/02/china-population-control-two-child-policy.

were already around in the nineteenth century. Victorian morality was in many ways a placeholder for conventional bourgeois morality in a culture that had largely abandoned both Aristotelian and Christian views that connected sex to marriage and procreation in its sexual beliefs and behaviors.[10] Advancing contraceptive technologies simply enabled and extended this ongoing abandonment. Yet, it was oral contraception, developed in the latter part of the twentieth century, that served as one of the main catalysts behind this burgeoning Revolution while taking it to a new level.[11] The introduction of "the pill" produced skyrocketing rates of extramarital sex, unwed pregnancy, divorce, and abortion.

As Mary Eberstadt has shown, this revolution inflicted harm differently across groups in the societies it impacted.[12] The most deeply affected were the most vulnerable—children. Most obviously and horribly afflicted were the millions of preborn children killed through abortions, the

---

[10]   This is the argument of Michael Hannon, "Against Heterosexuality," *First Things*, no. 241 (March 1, 2014): 27–34, www.firstthings .com/article/2014/03/against-heterosexuality. Hannon builds in a number of ways on the analysis of Michel Foucualt, *Histoire de la sexualité; Vol I: La Volonté de savoir* (Paris: Gallimard, 1976).

[11]   As noted in the previous chapter, these same technologies also helped to redirect the burgeoning women's movement of the 1960s away from many of its initial goals of greater educational and economic opportunities for women (including mothers) in the public sphere toward greater acceptance of non-marital sex, contraception, and abortion as keys to women's equality with men. Sue Ellen Browder's book *Subverted* documents and provides an inside look at this redirection.

[12]   This is the argument of much of her book *Adam and Eve after the Pill: Paradoxes of the Sexual Revolution* (San Francisco: Ignatius, 2012), esp. 36–93.

overwhelming majority of which were performed for reasons other than the health or life of the mother.[13] Many children whose parents chose life for them would later face the trauma inflicted by widespread divorce, which social scientific research indicates is devastating to children at any age—including in adulthood.[14] Finally, there is the ongoing sexualization of children by the pornography industry as well as media and entertainment.

Young people on many college campuses, face an aggressive and alcohol-fueled hook-up culture that has largely replaced dating in many quarters.[15] In this environment, students engage in some form of sexual activity, in part, in order to get to know one another or simply as something to do socially. Catholic universities, including those with strong Catholic identities are not immune to the operation and effects of this destructive subculture.[16] The objectifica-

---

[13]   The National Right to Life Committee, the oldest pro-life organization in the United States, estimated on the eve of the forty-eighth anniversary of the *Roe v. Wade* decision in 2021 that some 62.5 million babies had been killed through legal abortion. See Randall O'Bannon, "62,502,904 Babies Have Been Killed in Abortions Since Roe v. Wade in 1973," Life News, January 18, 2021, https://www.lifenews.com/2021/01/18/62502904-babies -have-been-killed-in-abortions-since-roe-v-wade-in-1973/.

[14]   See the findings described in Judith S. Wallerstein & Sandra Blakeslee, *Second Chances: Men, Women, & Children a Decade after Divorce* (New York: Ticknor & Fields [Houghton Mifflin], 1989). It also chronicles the harms inflicted on adults who divorce.

[15]   Eberstadt dubs this campus hook-up culture "Toxic U." See Eberstadt, *Adam and Eve*, 78–93.

[16]   For a thoughtful and in-depth examination of different forms of hook-up culture on various Catholic campuses, see Jason King, *Faith with Benefits: Hookup Culture on Catholic Campuses* (New York: Oxford, 2017).

tion of others bred by these kinds of practices is reinforced and compounded among young people by pornography.

According to Eberstadt, men have been infantilized by the Sexual Revolution. No longer needing to commit themselves to women in marriage to gain sexual access to them, men do not have to take responsibility for themselves and their sexual behavior. Contraception and abortion promise sex, free of consequences. If cohabitation, dating, or simply hooking up with actual women is too burdensome, men can satisfy their sexual needs virtually by simply consuming widely available pornography.[17] As a result, many men live in a kind of perpetual adolescence in which they avoid the maturation wrought by commitment—a perverse kind of Neverland enabled by the culture awash in sexual outlets.

Women, who had been promised empowerment by the sexual liberation widely promoted by second wave feminism, have also been among the Sexual Revolution's victims. Even while their political and economic power, as well as control over their fertility, have grown in recent decades, women's happiness relative to men's has declined in social scientific studies. Surveying the modern landscape of women who either eschew marriage or choose it only to be dissatisfied within it, Eberstadt argues that contemporary women suffer from "romantic want in a time of sexual plenty."[18] This is a paradox for which second wave feminism has no explanation.

Pope St. Paul VI's warnings in *Humanae vitae*, no. 17, concerning widespread adoption of contraception—a lowering of moral standards, greater moral confusion among the

---

17   See Eberstadt, *Adam and Eve*, 54–65.
18   Ibid., 53; see also pp. 36–53.

young, a loss of respect on the part of men for women, and the danger of government coercion in forced programs of contraception and sterilization—while visionary in their day, seem understated in retrospect. Social scientists have shown that the prophetic nature of these predictions as they have been more than vindicated by even secular social scientific measures.[19] Nevertheless, what Pope Paul VI did not foresee, and his teaching's proponents have not fully explored, is the impact of the Sexual Revolution on our understanding of sexual difference itself.

Effectively severing the longstanding theological, cultural, and social bonds between marriage, sex, and childbearing, the Sexual Revolution has given us sterile sex (backstopped by abortion), childless marriage, and—with an assist from assisted reproductive technologies—asexual reproduction. The shared fruitfulness of male and female that enables them to receive the gift of a child is thus rendered unimportant— peripheral to both sexual activity and the people who engage in it. What Paul VI identified as the "unitive" meaning of the conjugal act is reduced to mere pleasure to which the opposite sex and ultimately one's own sex becomes unimportant. The line from the pill to Obergefell, which illustrates the change in our social conception of marriage, is, therefore, not difficult to trace.

More difficult to discern, perhaps, is the impact of the Sexual Revolution on personal identity. If both sexual difference and the capacity for procreation are intrinsic to the person, as Scripture and the teaching of the Church affirm, it stands

---

19   See "The Vindication of *Humanae Vitae*," in Eberstadt, *Adam and Eve*, 134–58.

to reason that its cultural relativization will deeply impact the self-conception of those affected it.[20] Thus, there may be some connection between this destabilization of the sense of self as an embodied person and the rise in "rapid onset" gender dysphoria mentioned in chapter two. And, as discussed in that same chapter, there is a growing impulse to employ medical technology to render individuals with gender dysphoria sterile in the process of cosmetically reconfiguring them to take on the appearance of the opposite sex despite strong evidence for negative psychological and medical outcomes for those who choose to "transition."[21] Mary Eberstadt argues that the fracturing of the family caused by the Sexual Revolution has caused people to look for new places to "belong," giving further impetus to identity politics and accounting for some of the venom with which people respond when they believe that their group is being attacked.[22]

---

[20]   Another person who has begun to trace the impact of contraception along with gender theory on personal identity is Abigail Favale. See, for example, her thoughtful piece "The Eclipse of Sex by the Rise of Gender," *Church Life Journal* (March 1, 2019): https://churchlifejournal.nd.edu/articles/the-eclipse-of-sex-by-the-rise-of-gender/; hereinafter Favale, "The Eclispse of Sex by the Rise of Gender."

[21]   See the discussion in chapter two and the data found in Lawrence R. Meyer and Paul R. McHugh, "Sexuality and Gender," and Ryan Anderson, *When Harry Became Sally.*

[22]   See Eberstadt, *Primal Screams: How the Sexual Revolution Created Identity Politics* (West Conshohocken, PA: Templeton Press, 2019).

The Technological Revolution

A third revolution transforming the world in which we live is the ongoing explosion of technology. Like the Industrial Revolution, this expansion of technology has both positive and negative effects in our world. For example, information and communication technologies have made the world smaller, enabling instant contact between people in different corners of the globe. It has also made it possible for many businesses and schools in wealthy countries to continue operation in the midst of a global shutdown during the COVID-19 pandemic. Yet, this same technology can distance people living under the same roof from one another as they withdraw from actual human contact to be alone with their devices. The pervasiveness of this technology is altering patterns of oral and written communication and relational dynamics of all kinds in ways that we are only beginning to study and understand.[23]

Even though technology's total impact on the world is still developing, we have identified its darker side, which has furthered the reach of the Sexual Revolution and gender ideology: contraception, pornography, assisted reproductive technology, and chemical and surgical gender transitioning procedures. These assaults on the family will be addressed more thoroughly here, with the exception of contraception, which was addressed earlier.

---

[23]   For thoughtful studies of this ongoing impact, see Albert Borgmann, *Holding on to Reality: The Nature of Information at the Turn of the Millennium* (Chicago: University of Chicago Press, 1999), and Albert Borgmann, "The force of wilderness within the ubiquity of cyberspace," *AI & Society*, 32, no. 2 (2017): 261–265.

While the production of pornography has a long and undistinguished place in human history, the ever-widening expansion of its cultural reach has been enabled by technology. The invention of photography in the 1830s and motion pictures by the end of the same century were quickly put to use in the production of pornographic images. Full-scale pornographic films were available by the 1920s and became much more widely available in the acceleration of the Sexual Revolution unleashed in the 1960s. The creation of videocassettes and the video boom of the 1980s made such materials widely available in local video stores and more common in people's homes. The emergence of the internet in the following decade has put pornographic images and media just clicks away on millions of devices in households around the world. This epidemic has left worldwide carnage in its wake, desensitizing and sexualizing children,[24] destroying marriages,[25] and trapping people within destructive behaviors and sexual addiction.[26] Pornography made available through

---

[24]   Focus on the Family estimates that the average of first exposure to pornography in households with devices that connect to the Internet is now eight years old. See Ryan Rice, "4 Ways to Respond to Pornography," Lifeway Research, October 11, 2018, https://lifewayresearch.com/2018/10/11/4-ways-to-respond-to-pornography/.

[25]   Research in recent decades has found that excessive use of compulsive pornography was involved in almost sixty percent of divorce cases in the U.S. For an overview, see Monica Gabriel Marshall, "Divorce Lawyers Say This Is Why Marriages Are Falling Apart," Verily, July 28, 2017, https://verilymag.com/2017/07/causes-of-divorce-effects-of-watching-pornography.

[26]   For an overview of the harms wrought by pornography from the framework of Catholic teaching and pastoral strategies to respond to it, see the USCCB's 2015 Pastoral Letter, *Create in Me a Clean*

information technology has effectively taken the ideology of the Sexual Revolution that separated marriage, sex, and children and weaponized it into a form that is genuinely pervasive, permeating our culture and everything in it like a toxic fog. Pornography impacts both individuals and the wider culture. Within individuals, it creates habits of regarding oneself and others as objects—things—rather than persons. People become accustomed to abstracting from the person or persons before them and seeing a sexual commodity.[27] These intellectual and moral "habits" that pornography creates in its users encourage the dissociation of the body and sex from identity, which we have already seen at the heart of gender ideology. These habits then are reflected in the wider culture in the growing "pornification" of music, movies, television, video games, social media, and various applications.

In addition to the threat of pornography, assisted reproductive technology poses another great threat to marriage and the family. Although frequently described as a compassionate response to couples struggling with infertility, assisted reproductive technologies also distort the meaning of marriage, the dignity of women, and the gift of children.[28]

Heart: A Pastoral Response to Pornography. For an overview of pornography addiction and recovery from it, see Peter Kleponis, *Integrity Restored: Helping Catholic Families Win the Battle Against Pornography* (Steubenville, OH: Emmaus Road, 2019).

[27]   Maria Morrow argues that the habits created by the "narrative" that pornography creates are abstraction, commodification, objectification, and self-objectification. See her insightful essay "Pornography and Penance" in *Leaving and Coming Home: New Wineskins for Catholic Sexual Ethics*, David Cloutier, ed. (Eugene, OR: Cascade Books, 2010), 62–84.

[28]   See the instructions evaluating these technologies given by the

Such distortions have ramifications for our wider culture and our self-understanding. In many ways, these procedures are the inverse of contraception, tearing apart the life giving (procreative) from love expressing (unitive) meanings of sexual union in marriage. They exploit women's natural desire for motherhood, subjecting them to technological manipulation and objectification through procedures aimed at bypassing a problem rather than healing the disease of which female infertility is a symptom.[29] These forms of asexual reproduction also depersonalize children, treating them as products rather than persons who are gifts made in the image and likeness of God, whether by trying to create "designer children" through genetic screening or manipulation, or subjecting "spare" embryos to cryopreservation for later use or destruction in the name of scientific research. While perhaps not creating Shulamith Firestone's Marxist dystopia in which sexual reproduction is overcome by technology, these procedures, whether used inside or outside of marriage, further the Sexual Revolution's agenda of disconnecting marriage, sex, and children.

Finally, as discussed in chapter two, the use of medical and surgical intervention for the purpose of "gender transitioning procedures" harnesses technology to overwrite the body

Congregation for the Doctrine of the Faith in *Donum vitae* (1987) and *Dignitas personae* (2008).

[29]   For a thoughtful "new feminist" critique of these technologies and examination of NaPro technology as a better response to infertility ethically and medically, see Katie Elrod and Paul Carpentier, "The Church's Best Kept Secret: Church Teaching on Infertility Treatment," in *Women, Sex and the Church: A Case for Catholic Teaching*, Erika Bachiochi, ed. (Boston: Pauline, 2010), 121–40.

and its given sex. The available evidence shows that these procedures do not offer pathways to happiness or flourishing for those who utilize them as a means to deal with the pain of gender dysphoria. They use harsh chemical and surgical interventions to try to treat what is, at root, a psychological issue, leaving the deeper issues untreated and those persons with permanent damage to their bodies.

Moreover, using medical technology to satisfy demands that are not in the best interests of the patients themselves or conducive to their flourishing violates not only reason but also the basic aims and nature of medicine. In many ways, these procedures put medical technologies at the service of the currents of modern philosophy (e.g., existentialist, Marxist, or postmodern), which were discussed in the previous chapter. They promise the ability to overcome nature and God's designs by allowing the individual to forge a new identity independent of his or her biology and concrete historical context. Older concepts such as human nature, biology, and sex are defeated by technical praxis, enabling the individual to create or write a personal gender of his or her own articulation. Yet, this modern Babel, like its ancient counterpart, only deepens confusion among those who subscribe to it.

Technology is not evil: It is a human tool that can extend human dominion over creation. This dominion is integral to the image of God (see Gn 1:26, 28), enabling human beings to act as God's stewards within creation. Yet, this dominion is always subject to God who has designed creation and, in His loving providence, holds it in being. We are placed within creation to "cultivate and care for it" (Gn 2:15)—not to dominate, exploit, or remake it. These limits on human dominion extend both to the natural world—our "common home," as Pope Francis calls it[30]—and ourselves as creatures. As Pope St. John Paul II also reminded us, our technology often races ahead of our moral and ethical development, leaving us threatened by unintended harms we inflict on our planet and ourselves by pursuing technologies we have not adequately thought out.[31] Our current contraceptive dependence, pornography epidemic, reliance on assisted reproductive technologies, and use of aggressive medical and surgical techniques as treatments for gender dysphoria provide current examples of such technologically delivered self-harm.

Covenant Fidelity in a Fallen World

While Scripture begins and ends with weddings, the picture of marriage found between these bookends is not always so hopeful. God's covenant people in the Old Testament struggled to keep faith in the One who had chosen them as His own. Called out of the idolatry of surrounding Gentile nations to worship the Lord of heaven and earth, Israel often turned to the powerless idols of its neighbors. For prophets such as Hosea, Jeremiah, and Ezekiel, this was tantamount to His people adulterating their covenant with Him, giving themselves to lovers who were not their Lord (see Hos 1–4; Jer 2–3, 30–31; Ez 16, 23). This is why both idolatry and adultery were termed "the great sin" (ḥăṭā·'āh ḡəḏōlāh) in the

---

[30] See his encyclical letter on the environment, *Laudato si': On Care for Our Common Home* (2015).

[31] See his encyclical letter *Redemptor hominis* (1979), no. 15.

Old Testament (see Gn 20:9, 39:9; Ex 32:21, 30, 31; 2 Kgs 17:21). Both were egregious examples of covenant infidelity.

In some respects, the prominent sins of ancient Israel resemble many of those common in our own twenty-first-century culture. Early Old Testament texts record the presence of polygamy among God's covenant people—even on the part of some its patriarchs (see, e.g., Jacob in Gn 29:15–30; 30:1–9). The prophets condemned sexual activity outside of marriage such as adultery (see, e.g., Hos 4:1–2; Jer 7:9–10). The practice of legal divorce was a common, though largely male, prerogative (see Dt 24:1-4)—a prerogative diagnosed by Jesus as symptomatic of the people's "hardness of heart" (see Mt 19:8). Israel also participated in some of the ritual prostitution and child-sacrifice of her pagan neighbors despite these things being forbidden by the Torah (see Dt 23:18; 12:31). These practices have their counterparts in our own culture of sexual promiscuity, the divorce industry, and widespread abortion.[32]

Yet, there are differences as well, and these differences are significant for understanding the emergence and momentum of gender ideology in the world. According to Jesuit Scripture scholar Paul Mankowski, Israel's understanding of the command to be fertile and multiply (see Gn 1:28) helped set its people apart from the *goyim*—the nations of the world surrounding them. The prohibitions against child sacrifice, homosexual practices (see Lv 18:21–23), incest

[32]   On these parallels, especially regarding Israel's participation in the fertility cults and child sacrifice of the surrounding cultures and our own pursuit of sexual license and abortion, see Patrick Riley, *Civilising Sex: On Chastity and the Common Good* (Edinburgh, U.K.: T & T Clark, 2000), 100–13.

and bestiality (see Lv 20:13–17), and contraceptive practices such as those of Onan (see Gn 38:8–10) were all extensions of the blessing and command regarding fertility given in the first account of creation (see Gn 1:28). These injunctions form what Mankowski calls a "curriculum of fecundity," designed to teach Israel to treasure the life-giving capacity of sex and the gift of children received through it.[33]

It is in relation to the gift of fertility that we can see some of the sharpest differences between our culture and the one which Old Testament teaching aimed to form in ancient Israel. The seismic shifts in our world's landscape unleashed by the Industrial, Sexual, and Technological Revolutions and their ongoing effects have destabilized the understanding of marriage and the family derived from human reason and divine revelation. In addition to its own immediate detrimental effects on the family, the Industrial Revolution's separation of home and work have undercut people's ability to recognize children as a blessing and gift from God. Instead, many people regard children as threats to the financial well-being of their family or to the health of the planet. The Sexual Revolution drove deep and expanding wedges between the realities of marriage, sex, and children, causing people to view them as separate entities that can be pursued in any order or in complete isolation from one another. At every turn, it has been a variety of technologies—chemical, mechanical, informational, and medical—driving these wedges deeper.

---

[33]   Paul Mankowski, S.J., "Fertility, Celibacy and the Biblical Vindication of Marriage," in Helen Watt, ed., *Fertility and Gender: Issues in Reproductive and Sexual Ethics* (Oxford: Anscombe Bioethics Center, 2011), 11–12.

The three revolutions considered in this chapter are not three diverse and unrelated events. When it comes to their impact on views of marriage, sex, children, and sexual difference, they form a complex and interlocking whole, undermining and destabilizing a Judeo-Christian vision based on Scripture. This destabilization affected both individual persons and institutions such as the family and the Church. This, in turn, allowed the effects of the various forms of modern thought surveyed in the previous chapter—the bitter and toxic waters of existentialist, post-modern, and Marxist thought—to flow much more widely. With human nature and its Author denied, people increasingly view the body as a blank slate—raw material with which to construct any identity they so desire. Sexual difference in the form of being male or female loses its telos without an anchor in fertility. Since fertility is increasingly seen as a problem rather than a gift and blessing, personal identity is seen as unrelated to the biological realities of being male or female. This is increasingly true not just of persons dealing with the clinical reality of gender dysphoria, but of whole groups within the wider culture who dispute the idea of a sexual binary with procreation as one of its principle aims.

Information technology also enables the construction and projection of a virtual self in the virtual world of the internet and social media. People can create characters, alter them, or inhabit multiple online identities. This reality reinforces and visually enacts for many people the claims of existentialist and post-modern philosophies that we make or construct ourselves apart from a stable human nature or a world that reflects the wisdom of its Creator. This digitalization of identity, when coupled with the apparent malleability of the body in the face of gender transitioning procedures, invites many people to view their bodies as just another surface on which to write an identity. The fact that these procedures, permanently destroy the capacity to give life as a man or woman does not trouble those who see fertility as largely a problem in need of a solution. Scripture sees sterility as a curse—a withholding of God's blessing. For many in our culture, it has become an aspiration—whether based on pursuing individual happiness, sexual freedom, or the health of the planet. It is no accident that Planned Parenthood is one of the largest providers of transgender health services with sixty-five locations that offer various transitioning procedures.[34] Given that Planned Parenthood is in the business of promoting and profiting from barrenness through contraception and abortion, this should come as no surprise.

Many of the idols to which the peoples of ancient Israel turned were those of the pagan fertility cults that surrounded them in the hope of securing the blessing of fertility for their land and families. Instead of seeking to obtain life, our contemporary idols seek to expunge it while undermining "fidelity," which is at the heart of the marriage covenant. In so doing, we reject "the one blessing not forfeited by original sin nor washed away by the flood."[35] The negative effects

---

[34]   Alexandra Desanctis, "Planned Parenthood Jumps Into the Hormone-Therapy Game," *National Review* (August 2021): www
.nationalreview.com/2021/08/planned-parenthood-jumps-into
-the-hormone-therapy-game.

[35]   Nuptial Blessing, The Order of Celebrating Matrimony (2nd edition, USCCB, 2016), Option 1, http://catholicweddinghelp.com
/topics/text-nuptial-blessing.htm.

of modernity's three revolutions surveyed in this chapter coalesce in an attempted coup against the Author of life and His loving plan. Yet, the vision of the heavenly Jerusalem who is the Bride of the Lamb in the Book of Revelation reminds us, in a way quite different than is often heard from proponents of gender ideology after the *Obergefell* decision, in the end "love wins."

CHAPTER FIVE

DEAD ENDS AND DETOURS

*Since the Lord has thus redeemed us through His own blood,
giving His soul for our souls, and His flesh for our flesh, and
has also poured out the Spirit of the Father for the union and
communion of God and man, imparting indeed God to men
by means of the Spirit, and, on the other hand attaching man
to God by His own incarnation, and bestowing on us at His
coming immortality durably and truly, by means of communion with God—all the doctrines of the heretics fall to ruin.*
                            —St. Irenaeus, *Against the Heresies*, 5.1.1

*Gnosticism is one of the most sinister ideologies because, while
unduly exalting knowledge or a specific experience, it considers its own vision of reality to be perfect. Thus, perhaps without even realizing it, this ideology feeds on itself and becomes
even more myopic. It can become all the more illusory when it
masks itself as a disembodied spirituality. For gnosticism "by
its very nature seeks to domesticate the mystery", whether the
mystery of God and his grace, or the mystery of others' lives.*
                            —Pope Francis, *Gaudete et exsultate*, no. 40

*The human body shares in the dignity of "the image of God":
it is a human body precisely because it is animated by a spiritual soul, and it is the whole human person that is intended
to become, in the body of Christ, a temple of the Spirit: "Man,
though made of body and soul, is a unity. Through his very bodi-*

ly condition he sums up in himself the elements of the material
world. Through him they are thus brought to their highest per-
fection and can raise their voice in praise freely given to the Cre-
ator. For this reason man may not despise his bodily life. Rather
he is obliged to regard his body as good and to hold it in honor
since God has created it and will raise it up on the last day."
—*Catechism of the Catholic Church*, 364
(quoting *Gaudium et spes*, 14)

Caro salutis cardo ("the flesh is the hinge of salvation')
wrote Tertullian in the third century.[1] What did he
mean by this statement? To answer this question, we have
to consider just how revolutionary was the proclamation of
John's Gospel that "the Word became flesh and made his
dwelling among us" (Jn 1:14).

The great philosophical minds of classical antiquity generally looked upon the body as a tomb or prison for the intellectual or spiritual component within the individual (the
soul). Hence, Plato labeled the body as "the prison house of
the soul," Senecca spoke of "the detestable habitation of the
body," Epictetus pictured himself as "a poor soul shackled to
a corpse," and Porphyry in his biography of his philosophical master wrote that "Plotinus, our contemporary philosopher, seemed to be ashamed to be in the body."[2] In Plato's
mystical dualism, the task of the soul is to liberate itself from

---

[1] Tertullian, *De resurrectione carnis*, 8, 3 (my own translation).
[2] For references for and analysis of these statements, see Frank Bottomley, *Attitudes to the Body in Western Christendom* (London:
Lepus, 1979), 157. He points out the correspondence of these
views to the growing eroticism and decadence of post-Homeric
art.

the body and its limitations. Aristotle modified this dualism with his doctrine of hylomorphism: the idea that the soul is the form of the body but remains superior to the body and survives after death due to its divine nature whereas the body does not. This contempt for the body was institutionalized in Roman society in which the body was often regarded as a commodity to be bought and sold (in slavery), an object of pleasure (in the raucous theater and in widespread prostitution), or an object of cruelty for the purpose of entertainment (in the various games and circuses).[3]

The Old Testament, grounded in the doctrine of creation, offered a more positive view of the body. The body, like all of created reality, is good—in fact, "very good" (Gn 1:31). Though made from the clay of the ground, the human person contains something of God's own life: "Then the LORD God formed the man out of the dust of the ground and blew into his nostrils the breath of life, and the man became a living being" (Gn 2:7). Elsewhere in the Old Testament, animals can also be described as "a living soul" (*ḥayyāh le nepeš*); however, only human beings have "the breath of life" (*nišmat ḥayyîm*) breathed into them by God. These terms do not so much describe discreet "parts" of the human person as in Greek thought but rather the whole person viewed from

---

3   For an overview of Greco-Roman attitudes toward the body in the early Christian period, see Bottomley 1–15, 157–58. A similar socio-historical treatment of the pagan milieu and the novelty of Christian ideas concerning the body can be found in Peter Brown, *The Body and Society: Men, Women and Sexual Renunciation in Early Christianity* (New York: Columbia University Press, 1988), esp. 31–32 and 432–42.

different vantage points.[4] The body or flesh (*bāśār*) of the human being is the basis of all relationships, uniquely so in the marriage covenant since through sexual union the couple become one flesh (see Gn 2:24–25). But the covenant with God also has an embodied component lived out through ritual worship and the moral demands of the Torah. The body can also denote the frail and mortal state of humanity before God. Thus, the Psalmist says of God, "He remembered that they were flesh, a breath that passes on and does not return" (Ps 78:39), a condition we share with the animals (see Eccl 3:19; Ps 49:13). Later Old Testament texts (e.g., Dn 12:2; 2 Mc 7) depicted an individual resurrection, further differentiating human beings from animals and underscoring the dignity of the human body. This idea of a resurrection of the dead was shocking to Greek sensibilities, as Paul learned in Athens (see Acts 17:32).

Neither Greek philosophy nor the Old Testament contain an inkling that God would become human in such a way that the flesh itself would become an instrument of our salvation. Joseph Ratzinger (who became Pope Benedict XVI) captures the shock of the Incarnation as proclaimed by the Church in the Apostles' Creed:

> This second article of the Creed proclaims the absolutely staggering alliance of *logos* and *sarx*, of meaning and a single historical figure. The meaning that sustains all being has become flesh; that is it has entered history and become one individual in it; it is no longer simply what encompasses and sustains history but a

4   See Ratzinger, *Introduction to Christianity*, 347–56.

point in it. Accordingly the meaning of all being is
first of all no longer to be found in the sweep of mind
that rises above the individual, the limited into the
universal; it is no longer simply given in the world of
ideas, which transcends the individual and is reflected
in it only in a fragmentary fashion; it is to be found
in the midst of time, in the countenance of one man.[5]

It is this *logos* that St. John proclaims "became flesh" (Jn
1:14) in the prologue of his Gospel. That eternal Word who
was with God and was God from the beginning (see Jn. 1:1)
has taken on a human nature comprised of body and soul in
Jesus of Nazareth.

However, the Christian proclamation extends even further: It is Christ's human body in His Incarnation, in His
Passion and death, and in His bodily Resurrection that is the
very instrument of human deliverance from sin and death.
Christ's body, as Tertullian eloquently put it, becomes the
hinge of human salvation. Or in the words of Athanasius:

> For man had not been deified if joined to a creature,
> or unless the Son were very God; nor had man been
> brought into the Father's presence, unless He had been
> His natural and true Word who had put on the body.
> . . . For therefore the union was of this kind, that He
> might unite what is man by nature to Him who is in
> the nature of the Godhead, and his salvation and dei-
> fication might be sure. Therefore let those who deny
> that the Son is from the Father by nature and proper
> to His Essence, deny also that He took true human

---

[5]   Ratzinger, *Introduction to Christianity*, 193–94.

flesh of Mary Ever-Virgin; for in neither case had it been of profit to us men, whether the Word were not true and naturally Son of God, or the flesh not true which He assumed.[6]

It is His glorified and risen body, received in the Eucharist, that becomes, in the words of the great second-century bishop and martyr St. Ignatius of Antioch, "the medicine of immortality"[7] for those who worthily receive it. The embrace of materiality to communicate divine life to us in the economy of salvation is extended in the other sacraments, which use not just bread and wine, but water, oil, and the sexually differentiated body itself (in Matrimony and Holy Orders).

In His Incarnation, the Son of God assumed a sexually differentiated (i.e., male) body. He did not just become "man" in the generic sense (*homo*) but "a man" (*vir*). This has implications not just for who can represent Christ sacramentally in the Church's liturgy, but for all believers—male and female. Saint Augustine rejects Platonic readings of both Genesis and the New Testament found among some of the Greek Fathers, which held that both the first and the second Adam to be androgynous. For Augustine, we are male and female in creation (see Gn 1:27) and will remain male and female in the resurrected state. He writes:

---

[6]   Athanasius, *Contra Arianos* II, 70. The translation is from the Nicene and Post Nicene Fathers series, available at http://www.ne wadvent.org/fathers/. Citations of Patristic texts are taken from the translation in this series unless otherwise noted.

[7]   Ignatius of Antioch, *Ephesians* 20.2. He would also describe his impending martyrdom in Eucharistic terms: "I am God's wheat, and I am being ground by the teeth of the wild beasts, so that I may prove to be pure bread" (*Romans* 4.1).

From the words, "Till we all come to a perfect man, to the measure of the age of the fullness of Christ," and from the words, "Conformed to the image of the Son of God," some conclude that women shall not rise women, but that all shall be men, because God made man only of earth, and woman of the man. For my part, they seem to be wiser who make no doubt that both sexes shall rise. For there shall be no lust, which is now the cause of confusion. For before they sinned, the man and the woman were naked, and were not ashamed. From those bodies, then, vice shall be withdrawn, while nature shall be preserved. And the sex of woman is not a vice, but nature. It shall then indeed be superior to carnal intercourse and child-bearing; nevertheless the female members shall remain adapted not to the old uses, but to a new beauty, which, so far from provoking lust, now extinct, shall excite praise to the wisdom and clemency of God, who both made what was not and delivered from corruption what He made.[8]

Christ's resurrection from the dead makes clear that creation, the body, and sexual difference will be perfected—not erased—in the new heaven and the new earth that we await at the culmination of history.

The Gnostic Temptation

Even before the last books of the New Testament were completed, a very alien philosophy began to infiltrate parts of the Christian community. It was immediately identified by a few

---

8   Augustine, *De civitate Dei*, XXII, 17.

spiritually alert Church members as antithetical to Christian faith. The author of the First Letter of John warns of "antichrists" or "false prophets" who do not "acknowledge Jesus Christ come in the flesh" (1 Jn 4: 1–3). The opening of the letter offers a commentary on the prologue of the Gospel, underscoring the tangibility of the Incarnation. The Word of God who existed from the beginning is "what we have heard, what we have seen with our eyes, what we looked upon and touched with our hands" (1 Jn 1:1).

Who were these false prophets and antichrists who denied that Jesus had truly come in the flesh? Modern scholars call them Gnostics. The term comes from the Greek word for knowledge—*gnosis*—because its adherents believed that they possessed a secret knowledge about the universe and the divine that could set people free. With roots possibly in Buddhism or in Near Eastern mystery religions, Gnosticism entered the Mediterranean world in the first century and encountered Neo-Platonism, Judaism, and Christianity. It took ideas and language from each and crystalized them into a mystical philosophy antithetical to Jewish and Christian understandings of creation and the Christian doctrine of the Incarnation. The first centuries of the Christian era saw an explosive proliferation of Gnostic groups, many of which claimed to offer the only true account of the secret saving knowledge that was at the heart of Christianity. Because Gnostic thought was malleable, these groups were chameleon-like in their ability to adopt and utilize Christian ideas, language, and writings. In the late first and second centuries, this made it genuinely difficult to distinguish Gnostic groups from orthodox Christians in the Church.[9]

But within this shifting and shadowy collection of diverse groups and ideas there were some common elements. At its heart, Gnosticism explained the universe through metaphysical dualism: spirit is good, and matter is evil and illusory. The material world was the work of an evil, inferior god who seeks to trap humans within ignorance and illusion. Because of the pervasiveness of evil, Gnostics largely eschew reason and rely on the secret knowledge they claim to possess to understand and evaluate reality and truth. Some humans have a spark of the divine (spirit) trapped within them that is capable of redemption. That redemption can only come through accessing the secret *gnosis* that the group possesses and, usually, by following a set of quasi-ascetic practices (e.g., eating foods that are high in light and energy and avoiding marriage or at least sexual reproduction). This would enable the divine spark within the Gnostic to ascend through the heavens back to the divine realm (*pleroma*) where it belonged.

This radical dualism did violence to the Christian faith when it attempted to assimilate itself to Christianity, spawning a host of heretical ideas that the Church condemned. The creator God of the Old Testament was identified as the evil god, and so Gnostic teachers like Marcion tried to expunge Christian writings that focused too much on the Old Testament. Marcionism led to the formation of the

---

[9] Much of our knowledge of these groups and their teaching in this period come from the work of St. Irenaeus of Lyons in his multivolume catalogue often referred to by its Latin name *Adversus haereses* (*Against the Heresies*) written around the year 180 A.D.

New Testament canon in the third and fourth centuries. Jesus (an ambassador of the good God) did not really take on a human body or die on the Cross—He only appeared to do so (the heresy of Docetism). For the Gnostics, the body was not just inferior to the soul, as in classical philosophy, but was actually evil and incapable of redemption. It had to be overcome. Likewise, marriage and sexual reproduction were evil since they furthered the work of the evil god by entrapping sparks of spirit in evil and dark matter.

This explains why the Church Fathers insisted on the centrality of the flesh in the Christian faith. Christ's assumption of human nature—soul and body—is integral to how He saves us. Against every Gnostic denigration of the body and materiality, Christianity affirmed the goodness of both and the integral role of the body—both that of Christ and the individual Christian joined to him in salvation.[10] Salvation is not about escaping materiality but about the healing and restoration of materiality—a theological idea enacted liturgically in the Church's sacramental life that uses material realities to not just symbolize but communicate grace. And it is not just Christ's body that is significant. The bodies of those joined to him in Baptism become temples of the Holy Spirit (see 1 Cor 6:19). For those who take a vow of celibacy,

10   For a perceptive treatment of Gnostic understandings of the body, see Michael A. Williams, "Divine Image—Prison of Flesh: Perceptions of the Body in Ancient Gnosticism," in *Fragments for a History of the Human Body*, ed. Michael Feher, with Ramona Naddaff and Nadia Tazi, volume 1 (New York: Zone, 1989), 129–47. For an overview of the centrality of the body in patristic soteriology and anthropology, see Gedaliahu G. Stroumsa, "*Caro salutis cardo*: Shaping the Person in Early Christian Thought," *History of Religions*, 30 (1990–1991), 25–50.

their bodies become a visible proclamation of Christ's saving work and His victory over death.[11] For those Christian couples who exchange wedding vows, their bodies become a sign of their overall unity in faith. As Tertullian describes in his moving letter to his wife:

How shall we ever be able adequately to describe the happiness of that marriage which the Church arranges, the Sacrifice strengthens, upon which the blessing sets a seal, at which angels are present as witnesses, and to which the Father gives His consent? How beautiful, then, the marriage of two Christians, two who are one in hope, one in desire, one in the way of life they follow, one in the religion they practice. They are as brother and sister, both servants of the same Master. Nothing divides them, either in flesh or in spirit. They are, in very truth, two in one flesh; and where there is but one flesh there is also but one spirit. They pray together, they worship together, they fast together; instructing one another, encouraging one another, strengthening one another. Side by side they visit God's church and partake of God's Banquet; side by side they face difficulties   and   persecution,   share their consolations. . . . Hearing and seeing this, Christ rejoices. To such as these He gives His peace. Where there are two together, there also He is present; and where He is, there evil is not.[12]

---

[11]   Peter Brown's *Body and Society* offers one of the most comprehensive treatments of sexual renunciation in early Christianity and the way it was understood in the Roman world.

[12]   Tertullian, *Ad uxorem* 2, 8. The translation is that of William P.

This bodily union enables the couple to receive the blessing of children that the Church Fathers see as the chief purpose of marriage. Though celibacy is regarded as the higher calling, marriage and sexual reproduction are decisively and continuously affirmed as good.[13]

This brief contrast makes clear the mortal threat that Gnosticism posed to Christian belief and practice. It undermined the goodness of creation and God's identity as its Author, the reality of Incarnation, Christ's bodily death and Resurrection, the goodness of marriage and children, and the hope of the future resurrection of the body, which St. Paul sees as integral to the gospel message (see 1 Cor 15). In rejecting the goodness of the body and the reality of the Incarnation, Gnosticism jeopardized the very concept of salvation: "For that which He has not assumed He has not healed; but that which is united to His Godhead is also saved."[14]

The other reason why Gnosticism has been a particularly dangerous heresy for the Church is that, like a weed whose root cannot be fully removed, it has continually sprung up again and again throughout Christian history. From the Docetists and Manicheans, who troubled the early Church, to the Paulicians, Bogomils, Cathars, and Albigensians of the Middle Ages, to the New Age spirituality and turn to

Le Saint in *Ancient Christian Writers*, vol. 13, (New York: Paulist, 1978), 35–36.

[13] Saint Augustine uses the image of Martha and Mary in Luke 10: 38–42 to explain this relationship. Marriage, focused on the demands of the world, is like Martha. Whereas celibacy affords more undistracted focus on the Lord, like Mary who sat at his feet listening to his word. See Augustine, *De bono conjugali* 8; cf. 1 Cor. 7:25–40.

[14] Gregory of Nazianzus, *Letter to Cledonius*, Epistle, 101.

forms of Eastern mysticism in the late twentieth century, Gnosticism has emerged in different periods and settings. Modern expressions of this heresy have appeared in Puritanism, Marxism, and Nazism.[15] And, most recently, it can also be found in contemporary gender ideology.

Gender Ideology as Gnosticism

Adhering to its basic dualist worldview, Gnosticism can absorb and deploy language and ideas from diverse currents of thought, sounding similar to them by using their ideas and jargon. This syncretism gives the heresy its chameleon-like quality, making it difficult to recognize in its own right. Thus, Gnosticism can often blend unrecognized into the intellectual and cultural terrain around it.

Despite these challenges, it is possible to see that dualism lies at the heart of gender ideology, which bears Gnosticism's many marks. Gender ideology views the body of a gender discordant person as a problem to be overcome. The true "identity" of the person is independent of the body and its expression of sexual difference. In some cases, this is seen as the soul or spirit of the person being the true bearer of identity that is "trapped" in a body with a "sex assigned at birth" holding it back.[16] Gender ideology delivers the secret knowledge as to how this identity can be liberated and expressed.

---

[15]   Thus Edward Feser, building on and extending insights of Eric Voegelin, makes these connections and others (e.g., to critical race theory and right wing conspiracy theories such as QAnon) in "The Gnostic heresy's political successors," *The Catholic World Report*, January 31, 2021, https://www.catholicworldreport.com/2021/01/31/the-gnostic-heresys-political-successors/.

[16]   See Favale, "The Eclipse of Sex by the Rise of Gender."

Those who oppose this path of liberation are trapped in darkness and ignorance and, therefore, have to be opposed or cancelled with fanatical zeal.

Yet, there are some distinctively modern features of this modern iteration of Gnosticism that can make it harder to recognize gender ideology for what it is. As we have seen, it takes ideas from distinctively modern and atheistic currents of thought: existentialism, postmodernism, and Marxism. There is no human nature created by God to be realized (existentialism), only a self-articulated meaning. There is no absolute truth expressed in the body or sex (postmodernism), only that which the individual performs or writes. From Marxism, this Gnosticism derives its focus on praxis or action—both political and technological. Politically, gender ideology is strident in proclaiming its own so-called truth and intolerance of opposing views, aiming in various ways to silence them. There is little or no room for a dialogue based on reason or available evidence. Those who question or oppose the gnosis offered by this ideology are attacked as homophobic and transphobic or cancelled altogether.

The most distinctive feature of this twenty-first-century species of Gnosticism is that its program of salvation is achieved through a unique blend of secular ideas and technology. As Eric Voegelin observed, modern atheistic variants of Gnosticism "immanentize the eschaton" by seeing salvation achieved in this world, not in some spiritual realm of divine light beyond the material universe.[17] This is the case

---

17   The phrase was actually coined by conservative Catholic pundit William F. Buckley, Jr. after reading Voegelin's *New Science of Politics* in which Voegelin wrote that "a theoretical problem arises . . .

with gender ideology, which promises its believers earthly happiness through self-expressive fulfillment, liberated from the constraints of an oppressive biology and social constructions of gendered selves or binary sex. There is no human nature to realize just as there is no God who created it. There is simply the self that must create and write for itself a gendered identity that opposes the one assigned at birth or a non-binary one discovered or self-fashioned.

The way, however, that this salvation is delivered for gender discordant individuals is through a distinctively modern application of technology. Nature in general and the human body in particular are seen as raw material to be reshaped and overwritten through an array of technologies. This can involve information technology to alter online profiles or identities as a person socially transitions. And it can involve an array of chemical and surgical technologies to physically alter the appearance of the individual. Tragically, the person's fertility, one of the great casualties of gender ideology's war on the body, is destroyed by being sacrificed on the altar of self-expression. Yet, that sacrifice is not unique to the gender non-conforming—it is widely embraced by the contracepting majority of individuals who are untroubled by the concept of binary gender. This serves to blur the lines between believers in the iteration of Gnosticism that is gender ideology and the wider culture shaped by the Sexual Revolution. Once sexual difference is severed from its ordering to

---

when Christian transcendental fulfillment becomes immanentized"; see William F. Buckley, *The New Science of Politics: An Introduction*, Walgreen Foundation Lectures, (Chicago: University of Chicago, 1952), 185.

marriage and children, what is left is the solitary-self in search of meaning and pleasure. Still, the eradication of fertility is itself another point of contact between this ideology and the Gnosticism that sprang up in the first Christian centuries.

The Dead End of Gender Ideology

To call gender ideology a modern version of Gnosticism is to describe it as a heresy. The threat of Gnosticism in first centuries of the Church first caused Christians to distinguish between orthodox expressions of the Faith and heresy. Heresy can be defined as "the obstinate post-baptismal denial of some truth which must be believed with divine and catholic faith, or it is likewise an obstinate doubt concerning the same."[18] To hold to gender ideology is to subscribe to ideas that are antithetical to the Faith taught and handed on by the Church. If someone does so without seeing or understanding this conflict, they can be said to be in material (or unwitting) heresy. Such a person is not morally culpable for the break in communion with the faith of the Church that holding these ideas creates (though they may have some responsibility for their ignorance of the Faith). If a person understands the conflict between this ideology and his or her Christian faith and chooses to subscribe to these views anyway, then that person is formally in heresy and responsible for the break in communion it creates.

Gender ideology attacks the foundations of Christian anthropology. It rejects the doctrine of creation that sees the world, the body, marriage, and human fertility as good.

---

[18]   *CCC*, 2089.

It rejects the reality of sin as a willed rejection of God and His authority over creation and the human being made in His image. It distorts the idea of salvation, turning it into a worldly endeavor achieved through human effort and technology. It thus removes Christ and His Incarnation, life, bodily death, and Resurrection from the pursuit of salvation. Instead of the transformation of the world through the gift of the Holy Spirit poured out at Pentecost and made available through the sacramental life and ministry of the Church, gender ideology aims to overcome matter and the body through an individual and concerted technological attack on the human person as a composite of body and soul.

One does not have to be a Christian to see gender ideology as a false and destructive view of the human person. An honest and rational look at the available evidence suggests that not all is well in this heaven-on-earth claimed by gender ideology proponents. Reason and science alone make clear that the sexually differentiated body cannot be so easily overwritten. The ongoing endurance of a person's genotypic sex despite the full range of gender transitioning procedures is a stark reminder that sex cannot be wholly erased from the body. The fact that a person who has fully transitioned must remain on cross-sex hormones for the rest of his or her life is an ongoing sign of the body's refusal to fully submit to this technological override. The continued presence of mental health issues, psychological suffering, and staggering rates of suicide for those who have transitioned, as described earlier, underscores that these "medical experiments" harm rather than help the patient, thus violating the true aims of medicine.

The "woke science" advocated by gender ideology proponents willfully overlooks abundant evidence that call both its methods and results into question. This is not good medicine or science in any real sense of the term. Instead, this theory offers what critics have called a kind of "Frankenscience" in pursuit of its own ideological ends.[19]

In short, both faith and reason clearly show gender ideology for the dead end that it is.

Other Detours: The Shadow of the Archetypes

There are other dualistic ideas that have entered our cultural discourse about gender that should be mentioned. And these also bear some marks of Gnosticism. A few ideas offer a less radically dualistic picture, drawing more heavily from philosophies such as Platonism. In other cases, there is an effort to harmonize aspects of gender ideology with the witness of Scripture or Christian faith. A complete treatment or cataloguing of these other dualisms is beyond this book's scope. Still, the more influential strands within the culture and Christian circles will be addressed here.

Swiss psychologist Carl Jung, founder of analytical psychology, is known for many things. His wide influence extends beyond the realm of psychology into philosophy, spirituality, and theology, especially in the area of gender. Jung posited that each person has an unconscious component in their psyche corresponding to the opposite sex.

---

[19]   This is the term used by Ed Condin and J.D. Flynn in their piece "Will Catholics be forced to fight 'science' with science?" *The Pillar*, January 29, 2021, https://www.pillarcatholic.com/p/will-cat holics-be-forced-to-fight.

Thus, in his view, women have an *animus,* and men an *anima* within them. In other words, women have a masculine side, and men have a feminine side to their personalities. For Jung, these were part of a larger collective unconscious shared by all human beings. Another aspect of this collective unconscious is masculine and feminine archetypes that are found in myths, stories, and fairy tales across cultures and that can manifest themselves in an individual's dreams. Feminine archetypes can include things like goddess, mother, queen, amazon, lover, or wise woman. Masculine archetypes can include king, warrior, magician, lover, or wild man.

The sources of Jung's thought are dubious and diverse. He was an early collaborator with Freud but broke with him as he turned in more mystical directions. He clearly drew heavily on Plato, for example, in his understanding of the archetypes. But he also drew quite deliberately on Neo-pagan, occult, and Gnostic sources in infusing his psychology with the flavors of these non-Christian sources of anthropology and spirituality.[20] This eclecticism, as well as his own interest, creates some obvious lines of connection between Jung and Gnosticism, both ancient and modern.

Jung's ideas have proven to be fertile ground for those seeking "spirituality" outside the confines of a specific religion, often existing in or alongside various forms of Eastern spiritualities that have expanded rapidly in the West. This includes spiritualities that connect themselves to gender. Many second wave feminist thinkers—both self-identified

---

[20]   See the analysis of Jung's thought and its influence provided by Richard Noll, *The Jung Cult: Origins of a Charismatic Movement* (New Jersey: Princeton University Press, 1994).

Christian feminist theologians and those who rejected Christianity as hopelessly male-dominated—adopted some form of goddess spirituality often connected to a pantheistic ecofeminism, thereby (wittingly or unwittingly) deploying another of Jung's archetypes.[21] These blend into a larger landscape of New Age, the occult, and Eastern mysticism where this goddess archetype can indicate anything from overtly pagan worship to self-help books for women.[22] A similar range can be found in the wider men's spirituality movement that also has turned to Jungian archetypes to explain male spiritual development. This, too, ranges from overtly pagan or demonic to pop psychology.[23]

Given all of this, the number of Christian theologians who see Jung's work as a valuable dialogue partner and have drawn on his work to construct a Christian anthropology or spirituality is surprising. These efforts include works by Protestant, Orthodox, and Catholic authors from across the theological spectrum. They can include anything from

---

[21]   The thought of Rosemary Ruether, mentioned in chapter three, is an example.

[22]   For some recent examples, see Judith Laura, *Goddess Spirituality for the 21st Century*, 2nd Edition (San Francisco: Open Sea Press, 2011); Sarah Robinson, *Yoga for Witches* (East Cork, Ireland: Womancraft Publishing, 2020); and Dara Goldberg, *Awaken Your Inner Goddess: Practical Tools for Self-Care, Emotional Healing, and Self-Realization* (Emeryville, CA: Rockridge Press, 2020).

[23]   These would include works such as Robert Moore and Douglas Gillette, *King, Warrior, Magician, Lover: Rediscovering the Archetypes of the Mature Masculine* (San Francisco: Harper, 1991); and Dagonet Dewr, *Sacred Paths for Modern Men: A Wake Up Call from Your 12 Archetypes* (Woodbury, MN: Llewellyn Publications, 2007).

a wedding of Jungian archetypes and creation spirituality[24] to more serious efforts to use them to read Scripture or construct a Christian anthropology.[25] The shadow cast by Jung across theology and religious studies is a long one.

An example of a serious appropriation of Jungian thought in Christian anthropology and spirituality is provided by the work of twentieth-century theologian Paul Evdokimov. Evdokimov was a Russian Orthodox scholar who lived and taught most of his life in Paris. In 1958, he published a work on theological anthropology and the gifts of women.[26] Like much of Orthodox theology, it is deeply informed by the Church Fathers and by the liturgy and is in many ways profound and beautiful, even if somewhat romantic in its depiction of womanhood. But what is disturbing about the work is its usage of Jung and his archetypes to characterize and organize the Christian tradition. Mary, described in quasi-divine terms as *Sophia* and *Theotokos*, becomes the feminine archetype, humanizing the masculine God of the Old Testament by giving birth to Him, while John the Baptist, the violent ascetic witness, becomes the masculine one.[27] Christ cannot be the male archetype since, like the first Adam

---

24   See, for example, the work of former Dominican and now Episcopal priest Matthew Fox, *The Hidden Spirituality of Men: Ten Metaphors to Awaken the Sacred Masculine* (Novato, CA: New World Library, 2009).

25   See Patrick Arnold, S.J., *Wildmen, Warriors and Kings: Masculine Spirituality and the Bible* (New York: Crossroad, 1995).

26   The original French title was *La Femme et le salut du monde*. It was translated into English by Anthony Gythiel and published as *Woman and the Salvation of the World: A Christian Anthropology on the Charism of Women* (Crestwood, NY: St. Vladimir's, 1994).

27   See Evdokimov, *Woman and the Salvation of the World*, 197–248.

and humanity in the resurrected state, He is androgynous, reuniting the masculine and feminine principles in Himself.[28] The unmistakable message is that sexual difference is a problem of this fallen world to be overcome. This idea is found in some of the more Platonic parts of the Eastern tradition (such as in Origen and St. Gregory of Nyssa) and is here revived with the aid of Jungian archetypes. Hence, the sexually differentiated body is the result of the cosmic rupture produced by the Fall and has no inherent sacramental value or eschatological destiny.

To the contrary, our Faith encourages us to look to the saints as models of what Christian manhood or womanhood looks like in a particular place and time, or to honor the Blessed Mother for her unique role in salvation history. We can and should learn from them and cultivate devotion to them. But, at the same time, the saints are real flesh and blood persons—not ideal types who exist outside of space and time in the manner of Platonic ideas or Jung's ahistorical archetypes that represent a psychologized version of them. Forcing Christian revelation into the framework of Jung's ideas does violence to a Christian understanding of the human person. It also opens the door to more radical forms of Gnostic dualism advanced by gender ideology.

Beyond the Binary: Over the Rainbow

There have also been efforts to accommodate aspects of gender ideology in Christian theology in an effort to broaden the concept of sexual difference. One such effort is to use the biblical category of eunuchs as a kind of *tertium quid*

---

[28]   Ibid., 210, 227–28, 232, 251.

(i.e., a "third thing")—neither male nor female—thereby showing that even Scripture does not conform to a strict gender binary. This approach has been advanced by Megan de Franza among others. Initially she used this category to ground a biblical understanding of people with intersex conditions.[29] In her recent work, she has been more willing to extend this category to self-identified transgender persons.[30] For de Franza, examining the biblical portrayal of eunuchs in the Old and New Testaments reveals them to be outsiders who are models of discipleship (for example the Ethiopian Eunuch whom St. Philip baptizes in Acts 8).

Besides wrongly asserting that the Theology of the Body of Pope St. John Paul II cannot accommodate the reality of persons with an ambiguous expression of sexual difference, de Franza's position offers a bad reading of Scripture and suffers from flawed reasoning. It places great emphasis on a handful of biblical texts and uses them to read the rest of Scripture instead of considering the larger witness of the sacred text grounded in the theology of creation. Further, as noted above, intersex conditions do not explode the sexual binary. Logically, the ability to recognize the existence of male and female characteristics depends on the existence of both sexes, even if some individuals have characteristics belonging to both of them.[31] The effort to use this biblical category to accommodate individuals who are gender discordant and

---

[29]   See the published version of her dissertation in *Sex Difference in Christian Theology: Male, Female, and Intersex in the Image of God* (Grand Rapids, MI: Eerdmans, 2015), 68–105.

[30]   See her essay "Good News for Gender Minorities," in *Understanding Transgender Identities*, 147–78.

[31]   More will be said about intersex conditions in the next chapter.

identify as transgender is more tenuous and fraught with even larger problems. As noted in chapter two, there is significant evidence that gender dysphoria is primarily a psychological disorder akin to body dysmorphic disorder. As such, it can be seen as a disorder like many others that are present in a fallen world—not an authentic manifestation of sexual difference. This biblical category cannot ground or justify the use of transitioning procedures to make oneself a eunuch (see Mt 19:12) whether for the Kingdom or in a quest for personal happiness. It is worth noting that the early Church forbade persons who took Jesus' words literally from being ordained.[32]

Other authors argue more directly for importing the whole of the LGBTQ+ rainbow into a Christian account of sexual difference. Some have drawn on the work of iconoclastic evolutionary biologist Joan Roughgarden, who argues against the "sexual selection" theory of sexual behavior advanced by Darwin and much of the science that followed him. According to Roughgarden, animal and human behavior is frequently driven by what she calls "social selection," which can accommodate a much wider array of expressions of sexuality and sexual difference. Her position is based on the presence of both sexes in plants and fish and flexible sexual roles in many species, which point to the "naturalness" of gender flexibility and homosexual behavior in the world around us. A rainbow of difference and diversity is what nature itself displays when it comes to sex. Her work

---

[32]   Ironically, de Franza notes the Council of Nicaea's prohibition of self-castration but largely ignores it in her analysis. See "Good News," 163.

has been cited and utilized by theologians seeking to justify alternative expressions of sexual difference and same-sex activity within the Church.[33]

Roughgarden's efforts to reshape Christian ethics by proudly planting the LGBTQ+ rainbow flag in the natural world is scientifically and theologically flawed. Others in the field of evolutionary biology have been sharply critical. That is unsurprising given that most of the work in evolutionary biology turns on the basic and widespread nature of sexual dimorphism as the driver for animal and human sexual behavior.[34] Roughgarden's proposal misunderstands the theological relationship between the world as it exists, the theology of creation, and the natural law as a source for moral knowledge. The world as we encounter it—both the natural world and the human world—is a damaged one. Just because we find something occurring in ourselves or the world around us does not mean it accurately reflects the Creator's design. The natural world can cause evil and suffering through disease, disorder, or disaster. In ourselves, we find drives and desires that are ultimately at odds with God's intention for us and our flourishing (which Christian tradition calls concupiscence). When Catholic moral theology refers to the natural law, it is referring to a set of inclinations

---

[33]   See, for example, the volume *God, Science, Sex, Gender: An Interdisciplinary Approach to Christian Ethics* (Chicago: Loyola, 2010), which was based on a symposium at Loyola University in 2007. Roughgarden's essay was titled "Evolutionary Biology and Sexual Diversity," pp. 89–104.

[34]   See, for example, David Buss, *The Evolution of Desire*, revised ed. (New York: Basic Books, 2003); and Helen Fischer, *Why We Love: The Nature and Chemistry of Romantic Love*, revised and updated (New York: Holt, 2017).

that we share as being members of a species and through the pursuit of which we find fulfillment.[35] To discern these inclinations, we must abstract from individual actions of members of the human species to the goods at which they aim. These inclinations are spiritual goods that we apprehend and pursue through the use of reason and in response to grace. The virtues enable us to pursue them consistently. This is a very different understanding of "the natural" than that produced by extrapolating from observations of animal behavior to what is "natural" and morally good.[36]

Discerning Difference

There is a double postscript to the story about our family lunch table conversation about gender and Jesus that I mentioned in chapter three. After her exchange with her younger sister, my six-year-old daughter turned to me and asked, "Dad, what are angels?" After thinking for a moment, I launched into an explanation about the nature of angels as pure spirits that I thought might be accessible to a six and a three-year-old. I stated that angels did not have bodies like we did, that they were spirits who lived in God's presence

---

[35]   On the inclinations of human nature, see for example Saint Thomas Aquinas, *Summa Theologiae* I–II, q. 94, a. 2. Pope John Paul II acknowledged that Saint Thomas's articulation of the natural law is the classic one that the Church has made Her own. See *Veritatis splendor*, no. 44.

[36]   For a longer critique of Roughgarden's views and their deployment by theologians, see John S. Grabowski, "Not Just Love: The Anthropological Assumptions of Catholic Teaching on Same-Sex Attraction and Activity," in *Justice through Diversity*, Michael Sweeney, ed., (Lanham, MD: Rowman and Littlefield, 2016), 615–37, esp. 621–27.

and served as His messengers. After going on for a few min-
utes along these lines, I stopped and asked if it made sense.
My precocious six-year-old didn't miss a beat: "Sure, Dad.
Angels don't have bodies—so they're just heads with wings."
So much for my effort to make spiritual substances intelligi-
ble to my children!

Some eight years later, my daughter and I were attending a
Mass celebrating a friend's fortieth anniversary to the priesthood. The church's sanctuary was decorated with images
of cherubs depicted as heads with wings. The fact did not
escape the notice of my then teenage daughter who elbowed
me in the ribs and said, "Hey, Dad, look! I was right."

In its own way, Gnosticism, both ancient and modern,
mistakes human beings for spiritual beings like angels. The
body is illusory or an obstacle to us spiritual creatures. Gender ideology teaches its followers that the body can be overcome or erased. We can have the freedom of being subjects
unencumbered by the constraints of the body—"heads with
wings." But such a view is both false and dangerous.

The fourth chapter of the First Letter of John opens with
an exhortation to discernment of spirits:

> Beloved, do not trust every spirit but test the spirits
> to see whether they belong to God, because many
> false prophets have gone out into the world. This is
> how you can know the Spirit of God: every spirit that
> acknowledges Jesus Christ come in the flesh belongs
> to God, and every spirit that does not acknowledge
> Jesus does not belong to God. This is the spirit of the

antichrist that, as you heard, is to come, but in fact is
already in the world. (1 John 4:1–3)

Ideas that undermine the reality of the Incarnation jeopardize the basic contours of Christian belief: the goodness
of creation; the Son of God's joining Himself to our human
nature (comprised of body and soul); the reality of Christ's
bodily death and Resurrection; and the ongoing role of
Christ's risen and glorified body in the sacramental economy
of salvation. But these ideas also call into question the value
of the flesh of those joined to Him in Baptism, the Eucharist, the communion of faith, and the life in the Body of
Christ. This is because of the intrinsic connection between a
Christian understanding of the human person and the most
basic mysteries of the Christian faith. An attack on one is
necessarily an attack on the other.

The flesh is indeed the hinge of salvation, as Tertullian
noted. The flesh of Christ is the instrument by which God
saves us and invites us into His own life as a communion
of Persons. His glorified risen body is the means by which
He communicates this life to us in the sacraments. But this
divine life takes root in and transforms us as whole persons—
soul and body. The body of the Christian is made a temple
of the Holy Spirit by Baptism and becomes a tabernacle in
the reception of the Eucharist. That earthen vessel (see 2 Cor
4:7) has an eternal destiny and, therefore, an inestimable
dignity. This is why St. Paul is emphatic in his teaching that
what we do with our bodies matters. Our deeds can express
the "works of the flesh" (Gal 5:19–21) and exclude us from
the Kingdom of God, or they can manifest the "fruit of the
Spirit" (Gal 5:22) and of a life in the Spirit (see Rom 8:1–4).

When St. Paul warns about the flesh (*sarx*) and its works, he is referring to the whole person under the domination of sin (*hamartia*)—not to the body. At the same time, St. Paul reminds us that our bodies are meant to glorify God (see 1 Cor 6:20), which can only be accomplished with the help of grace. Living out this gift of grace in our bodily behavior is the basic demand of Christian morality.

Ideas and philosophies that denigrate the body or view it as an obstacle and a hindrance to the spiritual life should be viewed with caution and discerned carefully by members of the Christian community. Authentic Christian spirituality does not aim to overcome or escape the body—it aims at the transformation of the whole person in the life of grace. Christian asceticism and bodily self-denial aim to transform not just the body and its appetites, but the soul as well. In a sense, the body becomes the mentor of the soul in such practices.[37]

If gender ideology represents the dead end of Gnosticism, then the turn to Jungian archetypes, the misappropriation of the biblical notion of eunuchs, and the alleged rainbow of diverse gender forms and sexuality are equally wrong paths. What then does an authentic Christian account of sexual difference look like? The following chapter will outline an answer to that question.

---

[37]   Peter Brown argues that this was the understanding of ascetic practices that can be found in the writings of the Desert Fathers. See Peter Brown, *Body and Society*, 213–40.

CHAPTER SIX

BEHOLDING THE MYSTERY: RECEIVING THE GIFT OF SEXUAL DIFFERENCE

The truth is that only in the mystery of the incarnate Word does the mystery of man take on light. For Adam, the first man, was a figure of Him Who was to come, namely Christ the Lord. Christ, the final Adam, by the revelation of the mystery of the Father and His love, fully reveals man to man himself and makes his supreme calling clear. It is not surprising, then, that in Him all the aforementioned truths find their root and attain their crown.

—The Second Vatican Council,
Gaudium et Spes, no. 22

*So they lov'd, as love in twain
Had the essence but in one;
Two distincts, division none:*

*Number there in love was slain...
Property was thus appall'd,
That the self was not the same;
Single nature's double name
Neither two nor one was call'd.*

*Reason, in itself confounded,
Saw division grow together;*

To themselves yet either-neither,
Simple were so well compounded.

—William Shakespeare,
"The Phoenix and the Turtle"

The man had intercourse with his wife Eve, and she con-
ceived and gave birth to Cain, saying, "I have pro-
duced a male child with the help of the LORD."

—Genesis 4:1

Scripture opens with a wedding in the second account of creation. And this wedding takes place in the idyllic setting of a garden. Having breathed "the breath of life" (Gn 2:7) into the man who he had fashioned from the ground, God places him in a garden He had planted in Eden "in the East" (Gn 2:8). The word Eden (*ēden*) in Hebrew means "delight" and can include connotations of sensual or sexual delight. Some of the imagery of the text (e.g., the nakedness of the man and woman and the presence of the serpent that figured in the fertility cults of Israel's neighbors) has led some to see this story as all about sex—sex according to God's plan and sex gone awry through human sin.

That conclusion is overstated. There is much more to the creation account than sexual activity—good or bad. Still, there is clearly a sexual component to the story. As noted above, sexual union is presented as an act that ratifies the covenant of marriage making the man and woman one flesh (see Gn 2:24–25). This union enables them to receive the blessing of children with God's help (see Gn 1:28; 4:1).

The text, however, also teaches us important lessons about God's purpose in creating human beings, about the world

that we inhabit, and about sexual difference. A look at the
imagery used to describe Eden would immediately remind
ancient Israelite readers of the Jerusalem Temple, the first of
which was constructed around the time of the text's composition. This would include the Temple's eastward orientation
(see Ez 43:1–4), which corresponds to the Garden's location
in the East making it symbolic of light and divine revelation (see Is 2:2–4, 58; Ps 36:10).[1] The river that rises in the
Garden and waters the surrounding area (see Gn 2: 10–14)
corresponds to the river of Ezekiel's vision of the eschatological temple (see Ez 47:1, 7–12). The gold and precious
stones found in the area around the Garden correspond to
materials used to decorate the Temple. The golden candle-
sticks of the Temple were stylized representations of the Tree
of Life in the Garden (see Gn 2:9; Ex 25:31–35; Lv 24:1–9).
The cherubim who guarded the entrance of the Garden after
the couple's expulsion at the end of Genesis chapter three
(v. 24) recall the cherubim who adorned the walls of the
Tabernacle and Temple (see Ex 26:31; 1 Kgs 6:29), guarded
the inner sanctuary of the Temple (see 1 Kgs 6:23–28), or
formed the "Mercy Seat" (*kappōret*) on the top of the Ark
of the Covenant where God's presence was thought to rest
(see Ex 25:18–22). Finally, the description of God "walk-
ing about" (Gn 3:8) in the Garden recalls the description of
God's presence in the sanctuary of the Tabernacle or Temple (see Lv 26:12; Dt 23:15; 2 Sm 7:6–7). This wealth of
Temple imagery serves to foreground the holiness of God's
creation and of His plan for human life. Clearly, Genesis's

---

[1]   The Tabernacle is described in Numbers 2:2-3 and 3:23 as sharing
this orientation.

creation text and its multifaceted imagery offers a deeper meaning beyond just sex.

The point is brought home further by God's directive to the man: "You are free to eat from any of the trees of the garden except the tree of knowledge of good and evil. From that tree you shall not eat; when you eat from it you shall die" (Gn 2:16–17). Far from the imposition of an arbitrary rule, the Israelites understood this restriction on their human freedom to be an invitation to a covenantal relationship whereby they responded to God's generosity with love. Addressed by God in this way, the man discovers himself to be, in the words of Pope St. John Paul II, "*subject of a covenant*" and "*partner of the absolute* inasmuch as he must choose between good and evil, between life and death."[2] The Polish pope also insisted that to read the stories of creation rightly we need to do so through what he called "the hermeneutics of the gift."[3] That is, we must interpret the whole of creation out of nothing and the existence of the human person as a gift springing from God's eternal and unconditional love. Through their understanding and freedom, human beings can understand their existence as a gift from the Divine Giver and thereby return gratitude and obedience to Him.

The means through which the first man—'āḏām—came to the realization of the gift character of his existence and his call to a covenantal relationship with God was through his body. Through his body, he encountered the world that God

---

[2]   The citation is from John Paul II, *Man and Woman He Created Them: A Theology of the Body*, trans. Michael Waldstein (Boston: Pauline, 2006), 6:2, 151. All references to the Theology of the Body catecheses will be to this edition.

[3]   John Paul II, *Man and Woman*, 13:2, 179.

made for him. In God's creation of animals and the man's naming of them (see Gn 2:19–20), he came to recognize the uniqueness of his existence as a person. Only his body (and later that of the woman) expresses or reveals the reality of a person. After all, the animals, too, were creatures of God, which had value and purpose, but they were not self-aware subjects capable of making free choices. So, only the human body reflected the reality of a person and the full measure of God's gift within creation. In this sense, the solitude of the first man was also a gift, enabling him to rightly interpret the beauty of creation, his own place in it, and his call to respond to God. This ability is true not only of the first man, but of every human being—man or woman.

But this solitude was also an existential problem. God Himself declares: "It is not good for the man to be alone" (Gn 2:18). In the current canonical shape of the text, juxtaposed against the repeated refrain of the first creation account that everything God made was "good" or "very good," the state-ment is stunning. What the text highlights as "not good" is that *'ādām* is alone. In this state, he cannot realize himself or fulfill all of God's purposes for him—he is not designed to be a solitary being and cannot flourish as one.

God's proposed solution to this problem is to create a "helper suited" *('êzer kənegdōw)* to him (Gn 2:18). While in contemporary English the word "helper" can have con-notations of being secondary or subordinate, this is not true of the original Hebrew. A "helper" is one who gives aid or assists in realizing one's mission or purpose. Oftentimes, the term is applied to God as the "help" of Israel or of the righ-teous (see, e.g., Ex 18:4; Dt 33:7, 29; Ps 20:3; 33:20; 70:5;

89:19; 115:9, 10, 11; 121:2; 124:8; 146:5; Hos 13:9). The helper whom God will give in the creation of woman will enable *'āḏām* to realize his own humanity. She will also help him to realize the meaning of his own body. That is to say she complements him.

Sexual Complementarity

Looking at the two creation stories (Genesis 1:1–2:4 and Genesis 2:4–3:24) together reveals a number of distinct senses in which men and women may be said to be complementary. Both accounts of creation offer strong affirmations of the basic equality of the sexes in their fundamental humanity and in their creation in the image of God. Men and women together are designated priest stewards of creation by the first creation account, exercising dominion in creation (see Gn 1:26, 28) and finding fulfillment in the Sabbath worship of the seventh day (see Gn 2:1–3).

Within this basic equality, these texts also affirm a variety of ways in which men and women might be said to be complementarity to one another. The first might be called a complementarity of "totality"—the idea articulated in the first creation account that humankind (*'āḏām*) is only complete as male and female (see Gn 1:27). A second could be described as "procreative" complementarity—that is, the way in which the bodily differences of male and female (*zāḵār* and *nəqêḇāh*) enable them to receive the blessing of fertility (see Gn 1:28). A third could be called the complementarity of "alterity"—the way in which the threshold of solitude is crossed by going out from oneself to others. We realize our humanity in fellowship and friendship, and we do so as embodied persons. We become an "I" when we recognize and give ourselves to a "Thou" (see Gn 2:18, 23). To integrate the teaching of the two accounts and to employ the language of Pope St. John Paul II, *man became the image of God not only through his own humanity, but also through the communion of persons.*[4] A fourth could be called "spousal complementarity," which adds to the previous idea the dimension of the sexually differentiated body and the way in which this makes possible the covenant of marriage. This form of complementarity becomes clear when we consider the wealth of covenantal language and imagery in Genesis 2:21–25.

Reflecting on these texts and the realties to which they point, Catholic philosophers and theologians articulated the idea of complementarity. In her historical research, Sr. Prudence Allen locates the first fully articulated example of the theory (although not the term) in the work of St. Hildegard of Bingen in the twelfth century.[5] The idea emerged more clearly in the experiential personalism of twentieth-century Catholic converts such as Edith Stein and Dietrich von Hildebrand.[6] From this discussion, the concept made its way into magisterial teaching. One can find the term or equivalents of it in speeches of Popes Ven. Pius XII and St. John

4   John Paul II, *Man and Woman*, 9:3, 163 (emphasis in original).
5   See Prudence Allen, *The Concept of Woman, Volume 1: The Aristotelian Revolution, 750 B.C. – A. D. 1250* (Grand Rapids, MI: Eerdmans, 1997), 292–314, 408.
6   For a more complete overview of these thinkers and their influence on Karol Wojtyla/Pope John Paul II, see the excellent study by Prudence Allen, RSM, "Man-Woman Complementarity: The Catholic Inspiration," *Logos* 9, no. 3 (2006): 87–108.

XXIII, the documents of the Second Vatican Council, and Pope St. Paul VI, and it would be developed further in the long and fruitful pontificate of Pope St. John Paul II. Complementarity, for John Paul II, pertains to the very existence and self-awareness of the person:

> The knowledge of man passes through masculinity and femininity, which are, as it were, two incarnations of the same metaphysical solitude before God and the world— *two reciprocally completing ways of "being a body" and at the same time of being human*—as two complementary dimensions of self-knowledge and self-determination and, at the same time, *two complementary ways of being conscious of the meaning of the body.*[7]

His mature position would extend this complementarity to every dimension of the human person: "Womanhood and manhood are complementary *not only from the physical and psychological points of view,* but also from the *ontological.*"[8] The Vatican's position paper for the 1995 Beijing Conference differentiated this reality further, speaking of a "*biological, individual, personal, and spiritual complementarity.*"[9] In other words, the sexual complementarity of the male and female body points to complementary differences through the whole of the human personality. We do not just differ in our bodies; we differ our souls as well. As we will see below, the Church teaches that men and women have unique gifts

---

7   John Paul II, *Man and Woman* 10:1, 166 (emphasis in original).
8   John Paul II, *Letter to Women* (1995), no. 7 (emphasis in original).
9   John Paul II, *Holy See's Position Paper for Beijing* (August 25, 1995), 1.1 (emphasis in original).

and aptitudes that enable them to come together to create a family and to shape the wider culture. It is these differences that orient men and women toward one another and make them capable of giving themselves to each other in the covenant of marriage.

The Spousal Meaning of the Body

The notion of complementarity bespeaks a kind of teleology of the body. The body can be likened to a compass that provides the person with a basic direction in life. To read the compass rightly and navigate by it, one needs the further "map" of revelation provided in Scripture and Tradition. Divine Revelation clarifies that the world and the human person must be understood through the lens of gift—what Pope St. John Paul II referred to as "the hermeneutics of the gift." But what is the telos at which the body points? In the language of the Second Vatican Council, it too involves the language of gift: "Man, who is the only creature on earth which God willed for itself, cannot fully find himself except through a sincere gift of himself."[10] As a composite of body and soul, such a gift necessarily includes the body and its inherent maleness or femaleness. This gift orientation of the body-person manifested in sexual differentiation can be described as its "spousal" meaning. This idea also has deep roots in Scripture.

To the dilemma of the first man's solitude in the second story of creation ("it is not good for the man to be alone" [Gn 2:18]), God responds with the creation of woman who,

---

10   *Gaudium et spes*, no. 24.

unlike the animals created before her, proves to be the *'ēzer kəneg̱dōw* ("the helper corresponding" to him). Emerging from his sleep, the man declares his covenantal allegiance to the woman in marriage: "This one, at last, is bone of my bones and flesh of my flesh; This one shall be called *'iššāh*, for out of *'îš* this one has been taken" (Gn 2:23). It is noteworthy that until this point in the narrative the text has used only the more generic term *'āḏām* to describe the human creature made by God. For the first time in the text, we have the gender specific terms used.[11] The man does not here name the woman in the same way he named the animals in verses 19–20.[12] Rather, for the first time, he recognizes the meaning of his sexually differentiated body in light of her—he is not just *'āḏām* but *'îš*. Conversely, she too discovers the meaning of her reality as *'iššāh* (woman) in him. Sexual difference is thus revealed to be relational—ordering human persons toward one another. More specifically, it is disclosed as "spousal" since the whole account of the

---

[11]   This does not imply that prior to the creation of woman *'āḏām* should be understood as an androgynous being. The primary point of the term is to indicate the lowly origin of humanity made from the ground (*'āḏāmāh*—see Gn 2:7), which after sin becomes an indicator of mortality (see Gn 3:19). Further, the term continues to be applied to the male character in the story after the creation of woman, even functioning as a name.

[12]   The act of giving a name in biblical thought is a sign of superiority—to be able to grasp the essence of a thing and express it. The man does not "name" the woman in that manner until after their sin in 3:20, when he gives her a name denoting her function in creation: "The man gave his wife the name 'Eve,' because she was the mother of all the living" (Gn 3:20). But this occurs after God tells the couple that the man's rule over the woman is one of the effects of their rebellion against Him (see 3:16).

creation of woman in Genesis 2:21–25 employs covenantal language, and the text itself records the effect of the man's declaration to be marital (see Gn 2:24).

John Paul II builds upon this foundation in his analysis of the spousal meaning of the body in his catecheses on the Theology of the Body. Commenting on the covenant declaration of Adam in Genesis 2:23, he states:

> The body, which expresses femininity "for" masculinity and, vice versa, masculinity "for" femininity, manifests the reciprocity and the communion of persons. It expresses it through gift as the fundamental characteristic of personal existence. This is *the body: a witness* to creation as a fundamental gift, and therefore a witness *to Love as the source from which this same giving springs.* Masculinity-femininity—namely sex—is the original sign of a creative donation and at the same time <the sign of the gift that> man, male-female, becomes aware of a gift lived so to speak in an original way.[13]

More than merely its capacity for sexual self-gift, the spousal meaning of the body refers to the body's capacity to give and receive love in any state of life. It, therefore, applies equally to marriage and consecrated virginity or celibacy. It applies as well to the friendship and love lived in single life, even though the bodies of single people have not yet been given in a definitive gift of self. Thus, the Polish pope writes: "The nature of the one as well as the other love [marriage and

---

[13]   John Paul II, *Man and Woman*, 14:4, 183 (emphasis in original; the text in angled brackets was added by Waldstein from the Polish original of the text).

perfect continence] is 'spousal,' that is, expressed through the complete gift of self. The one as well as the other love tends to express that spousal meaning of the body, which has been inscribed 'from the beginning' in the personal structure of man and woman."[14] Pope Francis draws extensively on this understanding of the spousal meaning of the body in *Amoris laetitia*.[15]

Fatherhood and Motherhood

The spousal meaning of the body is ordered to fatherhood and motherhood. The biblical text is straightforward on this point: "The man had intercourse with his wife Eve, and she conceived and gave birth to Cain, saying, 'I have produced a male child with the help of the LORD'" (Gn 4:1). The text literally says that the man "knew" [16] (*yāḏaʿ*) his wife, and she thus conceived. John Paul II observes that this Hebrew idiom

---

[14]   Ibid., 78:4, 431.

[15]   This is especially true of the discussion of erotic love. See Pope Francis, *Amoris laetitia*, nos. 150–52; see esp. no. 151. He writes: "In this context, the erotic appears as a specifically human manifestation of sexuality. It enables us to discover 'the nuptial meaning of the body and the authentic dignity of the gift'. In his catecheses on the Theology of the Body, Saint John Paul II taught that sexual differentiation not only is 'a source of fruitfulness and procreation', but also possesses 'the capacity of expressing love: that love precisely in which the human person becomes a gift'." Other mentions of key concepts of the Theology of the Body in Pope Francis's Apostolic Exhortation can be found in the treatments of mutual submission in marriage (no. 156), consecrated virginity (no. 160), motherhood (no. 168; see also no. 173), the "language of the body" (no. 216), and education in chastity (no. 284). Suffice to say, this constitutes a deep engagement of the teaching of his predecessor.

[16]   Trans. RSV2CE.

is not a euphemism on the part of the sacred writer—it is a philosophically apt way to describe the "knowledge" spouses gain in giving themselves to each other in intercourse. In sexual union, they come to know each other more deeply not just as spouses (i.e, "man and wife") but as potential mother and father. He writes:

> We should observe that in Genesis 4:1 *the mystery of femininity manifests and reveals itself in its full depth through motherhood, as the text says, "who conceived and gave birth."* The woman stands before the man as mother, subject of the new human life that is conceived and develops in her and is born from her into the world. In this way, what also reveals itself is the mystery of the man's masculinity, that is the generative and "paternal;" meaning of his body.[17]

A husband and wife's self-donation in the marital act disposes them to receive the gift of life should God bless them with a child. In that child, the mystery of creation is renewed because new human life, made in the image and likeness of God, again enters the world.[18]

This insight indicates part of the biblical basis for what Pope St. Paul VI expressed in *Humanae vitae*, no. 12, regarding the "inseparable connection" between the unitive and procreative meanings of sexual union in marriage. It also reverses the cultural trajectory traced in the previous chapters, reconnecting the body, marriage, sex, and children to

---

[17]   John Paul II, *Man and Woman*, 21:2, 210–211.
[18]   See Ibid., 12:6, 213. See also John Paul II, "Letter to Families, *Gratissimam sane*," no. 11; Francis, *Amoris laetitia*, no. 168.

one another in a way that reflects God's design for human love, life, and fulfillment. Therefore, it creates an "anchor" for the sexed body and the person's identity as a man or a woman in the face of the confusion sown by secular philosophies, the Sexual Revolution, and gender ideology.

In light of sexual complementarity's impact on the whole person, it should not be surprising that the Church understands the orientation to fatherhood and motherhood as being more than a bodily reality. This awareness can extend the reality of the binary sex noticed by scientists and philosophers in classical antiquity that males reproduce by generating outside of their bodies while females reproduce by gestating offspring within their bodies. This observable phenomenon within most of the animal world has implications for differences in human parenthood. While noting the contributions of both parents in procreation, Pope St. John Paul II highlights the unique contribution of women:

> In the light of the "beginning," the mother accepts and loves as a person the child she is carrying in her womb. This unique contact with the new human being developing within her gives rise to an attitude toward human beings—not only towards her own child but every human being—which profoundly marks the woman's personality. It is commonly thought that *women* are more capable than men of paying attention to *another person* and that motherhood develops this predisposition even more. The man—even with his sharing in parenthood—always remains "outside" the process of

pregnancy and the baby's birth; in many ways he has to *learn* his own *"fatherhood" from the mother*.[19]

In other words, women's person-centeredness makes them uniquely capable of bonding with and nurturing children. These bonds between mother and child are formed and reinforced biochemically during pregnancy, childbirth, and lactation—realties from which men are excluded. Within the family, mothers provide a baseline of care and nurture that is often the foundation of the communion of love in the family.

Pope Francis echoes many of these insights of his predecessor, underscoring the reverence that should be expressed toward women's unique capacity to carry life and give birth. He also highlights the need for the distinct gifts of both mothers in the family and in society. He writes:

> "Mothers are the strongest antidote to the spread of self-centered individualism. . . . It is they who testify to the beauty of life." Certainly, a "society without mothers would be dehumanized, for mothers are always, even in the worst of times, witnesses to tenderness, dedication and moral strength. Mothers often communicate the deepest meaning of religious practice in the first prayers and acts of devotion that their children learn. . . . Without mothers not only would there be no new faithful, but the faith itself would lose part of its simple and profound warmth.[20]

---

[19]   John Paul II, Apostolic Letter *Mulieris dignitatem*, no. 18.

[20]   Francis, *Amoris laetitia*, no. 174. The quotation is from the Pope's own catechesis of January 7, 2015.

What of fathers? They too make indispensable contributions to their children's well-being. Pope Francis notes, "A father possessed of a clear and serene masculine identity who demonstrates affection and concern for his wife is just as necessary as a caring mother."[21] While noting the challenges posed by overbearing or absentee fathers, Pope Francis also highlights the value of what they give to their children through their mere presence:

> God sets the father in the family so that by the gifts of his masculinity he can be "close to   his   wife   and share everything, joy and sorrow, hope and hardship. And to be close to his children as they grow – when they play and when they work, when they are carefree and when they are distressed, when they are talkative and when they are silent, when they are daring and when they are afraid, when they stray and when they get back on the right path. To be a father who is always present." . . . It is not good for children to lack a father and to grow up before they are ready.[22]

Through their patience and their paternal presence, earthly fathers reveal the Heavenly Father's face and His love for their children. Contemporary social science corroborates the absolute necessity of a father's role in his children's formation. An absent father is a recipe for family and societal disorder. If women provide a foundation of nurture within the family, healthy fathers complement this by helping their

---

21   Ibid., no. 175.
22   Francis, *Amoris laetitia*, no. 177. The quotation is from the Pope's catechesis of February 4, 2015.

wives set boundaries (i.e., with discipline) and by promoting healthy risk-taking on the part of both male and female children.[23] Scripture highlights the unique role men have as teachers within their families, at times using the terms "father" and "teacher" synonymously (see Jgs 17:10; 1 Cor 4:14).[24] Even secular studies have captured the unique impact fathers make on their children in teaching and modeling the Faith.[25]

But what of those couples who are unable to have children? According to the Catholic Church, the vocations of fatherhood and motherhood are not limited to being biological parents. Infertile couples can exercise the fruitfulness of their love through adoption or through other kinds of ministry or service together.[26] Furthermore, those who are biological or adoptive parents are also called to exercise spiritual motherhood and fatherhood by educating their

---

[23]   See, for example, the data provided by neuropsychiatrist Luann Brizendine in *The Male Brain: A Breakthrough Understanding of How Men and Boys Think* (New York: Three Rivers Press, 2010), esp. 79–94.

[24]   See the excellent overview of biblical fatherhood provided by John W. Miller in *Calling God Father: Essays on the Bible, Fatherhood, and Culture*, 2nd ed. (New York: Paulist, 1999).

[25]   A study by the Swiss government conducted in 1994 and published in 2000 demonstrated that if the father in a family does not attend church—no matter how regularly his wife goes—only one child in fifty will attend church as an adult. But, if a father does go regularly (regardless of the mother's attendance), between two-thirds and three-quarters of those children will attend church as adults. See Tara K. E. Brelinsky, "Dads Make All the Difference," Catholic Online, https://www.catholic.org/news/hf/family/story.php?id=75859.

[26]   Pope Francis discusses some of these other forms of fruitfulness in *Amoris laetitia*, nos. 178–84.

children and forming them in the Faith.[27] In fact, all mature Christian men and women are called to spiritual fatherhood and motherhood in whatever state in life in which they find themselves. This reality can be observed most easily in the priesthood or different forms of consecrated life—states in life devoted to the exercise of this spiritual generativity. But it can also be lived out in other contexts by mature and generous adults who serve as guardians, teachers, or mentors. Any woman who nurtures spiritual life and fosters communion exercises spiritual motherhood. Any man who passes on the Faith by teaching or mentoring others acts as a spiritual father.

Given the gender confusion that exists in our society, it is worth noting that in the Church's understanding these vocations to motherhood or fatherhood are not interchangeable. Only men can be fathers—whether physical or spiritual. And only women can be mothers—again, whether physical or spiritual. These "roles" cannot be swapped at will or absorbed into an amorphous gender neutral "parenthood." Both the Church and social scientific data agree that children require both a father and a mother to flourish.[28]

---

[27]   For St. Augustine, the *bonum prolis* or the good of offspring (which he sees as the chief good of marriage) is not merely physical begetting but the joy and duty of caring for, loving, and educating children (humanly and in the Christian faith). See Augustine, *De bono conjuigali*.

[28]   See Francis, *Amoris laetitia*, no. 172. For an excellent overview of relevant social science data see D. Paul Sullins, "The Case for Mom and Dad" *The Linacre Quarterly* 88, no. 2 (2021): 184–201.

Nature vs. Person

Scripture and Tradition help us to understand that sexual difference is a relational reality, ordering us toward specific kinds of communion with one another. Sexual difference is directed to and realized in a particular way in the communion of marriage and family—both the natural family and the spiritual family of faith that is the Church. It makes us capable of being a son or daughter, a brother or sister, a husband or wife, or a father or mother, whether these relations are created by blood, sacrament, or religious profession.

Pope St. John Paul II often described the Christian family and the Church as the family of God with the same term he used to describe the mystery of the Trinity. These, he said, are a *communion personarum* ("a communion of persons") constituted by relations of self-gift.[29] Clearly, the language here is analogous. No human family—no matter how loving—can embody the total gift of self and eternal communion that exists between the Persons of the Father, Son, and Holy Spirit. And while Christian families and the Church share in this eternal communion through grace, they are still comprised of limited and sinful human members.

But what is the philosophical "weight" or status of these differences that orient us toward communion? The Incarnation makes clear that sexual difference does not divide humanity on the level of nature. If women have a nature distinct from their male counterparts, then as second wave feminist theologians have rightly asked, how can women be

---

[29]   See, for example, John Paul II, *Familiaris consortio* (November 22, 1981), no.15, and John Paul II, "Letter to Families, *Gratissimam sane,*" no. 6.

saved by a male savior?[30] It is only insofar as we hold that the Son of God assumed a human nature common to men and women, that he is the Savior of the whole human race. In the words of St. Gregory of Nazianzus: "For that which He has not assumed He has not healed; but that which is united to His Godhead is also saved."[31] More recent Catholic teaching and theology, responding more directly to anthropological questions raised by feminism has focused more directly on the Christological and Trinitarian language of "nature" and "person" as a way to account for the unity and difference of the human race. So, John Paul II writes: "[Man and woman's] unity *denotes* above all *the identity of human nature; duality, on the other hand, shows what, on the basis of this identity, constitutes the masculinity and femininity* of created man."[32] Therefore, male and female are two distinct ways of existing as a person within a common human nature. Both men and women are equally and fully human. There is no second-class sex. These distinct forms of personal existence are expressed through the two basic forms of human embodiment: "Masculinity and femininity express *the twofold aspect of man's somatic constitution* . . . and *indicate* . . . *the new consciousness of the meaning of one's body,*" which has a "*reciprocal enrichment.*"[33] This idea that there is one human nature that is possessed in two irreducibly different ways of being a

30   See, for example, Rosemary Radford Ruether, "Can a Male Savior Save Women?" in *To Change the World: Christology and Cultural Criticism* (London: SCM, 1981), 45–56; and Elizabeth Johnson, "The Maleness of Christ," in *The Special Nature of Women? Concilium* 1991/6: 108–16, esp. 109.

31   Gregory of Nazianzus, *Letter to Cledonius* (Epistle, 101).

32   John Paul II, *Man and Woman* 9:1, 161 (emphasis in original).

33   Ibid., 9:5, 165 (emphasis in original).

human person has been widely echoed in Catholic theology over the past few decades.[34]

Sexual difference is therefore an inescapable part of the embodied individual human being. Put more directly, sexual difference is accidental to human nature in general but essential to existing individuals. To grasp the distinction, a parallel illustration might help. Aristotle and St. Thomas Aquinas note that it belongs to the nature of numbers (in general) that they be odd or even. But any actually existing number will be only odd or even.[35] If one makes the number four to be odd, it is no longer four but a different number altogether. As John Finley observes, "Odd and even, while not mutually relational within their being, are difficult to understand and articulate apart from the other, in this sense resembling male and female, which are mutually relational in their being, not to mention in their intelligibility."[36] One of the things that this suggests is that, if such a thing were possible, a true "sex change" procedure that were to alter every dimension of a person's expression of sexual difference (including their genotype and fertility) would transform the person into a completely different person. Gender transitioning procedures that cosmetically reconfigure the appearance of a person's body and destroy their fertility in the process fall far short of this transformation of personal identity. Only God can make or remake a person that completely.

---

[34] For examples and references, see Grabowski, "Sexual Difference and the Catholic Tradition," 130–31.
[35] See Aristotle, *Metaphysics* 1.5.986a22-b1, and Aquinas, *X Metaphysics*, lect. 11 (2128).
[36] John Finley, "The Metaphysics of Gender: A Thomistic Approach," *The Thomist*, 79 (2015): 607.

But the human individual is a person—a "someone" and not merely a "something." Since "the body expresses the person," sexual difference communicates the irreducible uniqueness of the free human subject who is male or female. So, this difference can be understood as a created relation constitutive of personhood analogous to the divine and spiritual relations of paternity, filiation, and spiration that we recognize in the Trinitarian communion. And, as we have seen, this fundamental human relation is itself the basis of other relations at the heart of personal existence—being a son or daughter, a sister or a brother, a husband or a wife, a mother or a father.

This is a further instantiation of the Second Vatican Council's insight that the human person becomes intelligible in the light of Christ. The conundrum of sexual difference begins to become clear with the aid of the Christological and Trinitarian distinction of nature and person (understood relationally). Though as a spiritual being, God transcends biological sex, male and female who are made in the image of God have the call to communion inscribed in their very bodies.[37] The compass of the body points us toward the love that is our origin and our fulfillment.

Sex and Gender: Vocations, Gifts, and Roles

As noted in the first chapter, Pope Francis echoes the concerns about gender ideology raised by various Vatican diacasteries and by Pope Benedict XVI. In *Amoris laetitia*, no. 56, the Holy Father writes:

---

[37]   See John Paul II, *Mulieris dignitatem*, nos. 7–8.

Yet another challenge is posed by the various forms of an ideology of gender that "denies the difference and reciprocity in nature of a man and a woman and envisages a society without sexual differences, thereby eliminating the anthropological basis of the family. This ideology leads to educational programmes and legislative enactments that promote a personal identity and emotional intimacy radically separated from the biological difference between male and female. Consequently, human identity becomes the choice of the individual, one which can also change over time." It is a source of concern that some ideologies of this sort, which seek to respond to what are at times understandable aspirations, manage to assert themselves as absolute and unquestionable, even dictating how children should be raised.[38]

Pope Francis, however, adds an important further observation: "It needs to be emphasized that 'biological sex and the socio-cultural role of sex (gender) can be distinguished but not separated.'"[39] Hence, "gender" (or nurture) can be a useful way to talk about the manner in which culture impacts the way we think about difference, but it cannot be separated from the sexually differentiated body and the deeper metaphysical differences between men and women (i.e., nature).[40]

---

[38]   Francis, *Amoris laetitia*, no. 56, citing the Synod of Bishops, *Relatio finalis* (October 24, 2015), no. 8.

[39]   Francis, *Amoris laetitia*, no. 56, citing the Synod of Bishops, *Relatio finalis*, no. 58.

[40]   Catholic "new feminist" authors have argued that one of the intel-

One way to begin to think about the significance of this qualification in light of the analysis above is to distinguish between the vocations, gifts, and roles of the sexes. Only men can fulfill the vocation to be husbands and fathers—whether spiritual or both physical and spiritual. As noted above, only women can undertake the vocation to be wives and mothers—whether spiritual or both physical and spiritual. These states in life further specify and concretize the manner in which the fundamental baptismal vocation to holiness is lived out. They are, therefore, vocations within this more basic baptismal vocation.

Roles, on the other hand, are more expressive of cultural and familial assumptions about things that are appropriate for one sex or the other. Such roles can vary from culture to culture or change over time within the same culture. For example, many Americans in the mid-twentieth century believed that it was a man's "role" to go off to work while a woman stayed home and cared for children. These differing roles would not have corresponded to the same cultural assumption prior to the Industrial Revolution. In the pre-industrialized western world, men and women generally worked side by side on the family farm or in the family business. They also worked closely together in raising their children, even if they focused on imparting different kinds of knowledge or skills. Using Pope Francis's distinction, we could say that vocations are rooted in one's sex as male or

---

lectual tasks of our day is to articulate the intellectual basis for a "reunion" of sex and gender. See Barbara Voles, "New Feminism: A Sex Gender Reunion," in *Women in Christ: Toward a New Feminism*, Michelle Schumacher, ed. (Grand Rapids, MI: William B. Eerdmans, 2005), 52–66.

female, while roles are the gendered assumptions about how these get lived out in a particular culture. The first is more fixed, while the second is more flexible and, hence, is capable of change.

In the lives of the saints, some of them violated specific gender roles without compromising their basic vocation because of their particular culture's circumstances. Saint Hildegard of Bingen exercised what she described as a masculine office of preaching and teaching due to the weak and effeminate state of the clergy in her day. Saint Joan of Arc led French troops into battle and was executed by the English for witchcraft and heresy (in part because of the violation of gender roles). Yet, these roles did not undermine the spiritual maternity of Hildegard caring for her nuns or Joan for her troops. Saint Bernard of Clairvaux used bridal imagery to describe the love between the soul and God in his sermons on the Song of Songs. This fact does not negate the spiritual fatherhood he excised as a monastic reformer and teacher, nor does it suggest some kind of partially sublimated same-sex attraction on his part. This is another reason why it is unhelpful to turn flesh and blood saints into disembodied archetypes or read their lives through the lens of our confused gender politics.

What the Church has referred to as the "genius" or gifts of both sexes could be understood as existing between sex specific vocations and culturally shaped roles. They can be generally attributed to each sex as a group, but they will be lived out somewhat differently by individual men and women. Some of these gifts show up in social scientific research as propensities that are attributable to one sex or the other as a whole, while leaving room for individual variation in how they are expressed. As we have seen, recent Church teaching and "new feminist" theology has done much to highlight some of the distinctive gifts of women—for example, their "person-centeredness" that is enhanced by motherhood, their capacity to nurture life, and to build and sustain communion. [41] Less attention has been paid to the genius of men, but some theologians have begun to reflect more directly on this question. Christian Raab, building on the work of Walter Ong's important book *Fighting for Life*, calls attention to expendability, agonistic differentiation, and exteriority in the order of nature, and (masculine) self-giving, the militancy of discipleship, and being a sign of divine otherness in the order of grace. [42]

Deborah Savage, in an insightful analysis of the complementary genius of the sexes, explores John Paul II's study of the second account of creation. She notes that the man's charge to till and to keep the garden (see Gn 2:15; RSV2CE), his task of naming the animals (see Gn 2:19–20), the fact that he plays a role in introducing the woman to

---

[41]   See John Paul II, *Mulieris dignitatem*, no. 18, C.D.F., "Letter to the Bishops of the Catholic Church on the Collaboration of Men and Women in the Church and in the World" (2004), and Francis, *Amoris laetitia*, nos. 168, 173.

[42]   Christian Raab, O.S.B., "In Search of the Masculine Genius: The Contribution of Walter J. Ong," *Logos* 21, no. 1, (Winter 2018): 83–117. Expendability refers to the biological fact that groups of animals and humans can better absorb losses to males than females in regard to their reproductive success. Agonistic differentiation refers to the male propensity for contest and struggle to realize their own masculine identity. Exteriority refers to the male propensity toward objects and the world of work.

God and the things of creation, all point to aspects of the masculine genius. Specifically, this genius consists in the "capacity to know and use the goods of the earth in the service of authentic human flourishing."[43] Woman, she notes, is introduced into a world of persons inhabited by the man and God, pointing toward the feminine orientation toward persons (as opposed to the things of the world) noted by John Paul II earlier.[44] Savage insists that both sets of gifts are necessary for the flourishing of the family and the wider human society as a whole. These distinctive orientations of men and women as persons are reflected in the impact of sin on each sex. Men's relationship to the natural world is now marked by the burden of toil and resistance on the part of creation (see Gn 3:17–19). Women are burdened with pain in childbirth and a disordered relationship to their husbands (see Gn 3:16).

The Church has been clear in her recent teaching that these "gifts" do not tie sexes to rigid sex-specific roles in the home or society. The genius of women is needed in public life—in the worlds of business and politics.[45] The gifts of

---

[43]   Deborah Savage, "The Genius of Man," in *Promise and Challenge: Catholic Women Reflect on Feminism, Complementarity, and the Church*, Mary Rice Hasson, ed. (Huntington, IN: OSV, 2015), 129–53; the citation is from p. 146.

[44]   See Ibid., 139–40.

[45]   For example, in his 1995 Letter to Women, Pope St. John Paul II wrote: "Thank you, women who work! You are present and active in every area of life–social, economic, cultural, artistic and political. In this way you make an indispensable contribution to the growth of a culture which unites reason and feeling, to a model of life ever open to the sense of "mystery", to the establishment of economic and political structures ever more worthy of humanity" (no. 2). See also Francis, *Amoris Laetitia*, no. 103.

men are needed in the home to raise children and contribute to household tasks. Absentee fathers are one of the crises of our time and are another bitter fruit of the Sexual Revolution.[46] The Church is not advocating for sex stereotyping. A man who does housework or is a stay-at-home dad does not cease to be a man. A woman who plays competitive sports does not cease to be a woman. Abigail Favale draws on John Paul II's usage to illustrate the point:

> St. John Paul II's unique understanding of the terms "masculinity" and "femininity" could be helpful here. He uses these terms exclusively in reference to males and females respectively. Masculinity is simply the way of being a man in the world, and is thus uniquely inflected by each individual personality. Thus, when my husband, Michael, is caring for our children and cooking dinner, these are masculine acts, because they are being performed by a male human being. Similarly, my femininity is exhibited as much I my assertiveness during a staff meeting as when I am breastfeeding— because it is the person who is gendered, not the act or trait. This embodied, personalist understanding of masculinity and femininity reaffirms the meaning of the sexed body, without collapsing cultural stereotypes into natural categories.[47]

---

[46] See David Blankenhorn, *Fatherless America: Confronting Our Most Urgent Social Problem* (New York: Harper, 1995).

[47] Abigail Favale, "The Eclipse of Sex by the Rise of Gender," *Church Life Journal*, March 1, 2019, https://churchlifejournal.nd.edu/articles/the-eclipse-of-sex-by-the-rise-of-gender/.

The Church's vision is thus a nuanced one, recognizing a givenness of sexual difference rooted in the body as well as the uniqueness of the person who is male or female. But what happens when the bodily signs of sex are themselves unclear?

Intersex Persons and the Vocation to Love

The existence of individuals with intersex conditions does not itself explode the idea of binary sex in much of the animal kingdom or the human world. This can be established in a variety of ways. Writing in his 1960 book *Love and Responsibility*, Bishop Karol Wojtyla observed that everyone "belongs from birth to one of the two sexes. This fact is not contradicted by hermaphroditism—any more than any other sickness or deformity militates against the fact that there is such a thing as human nature."[48] This argument presupposes something like Aristotle's distinction between act and potency. The fact that one individual does not properly develop one of the characteristics of what it means to be human because of a disease or disorder does not mean he or she ceases to be a member of the species. Rather, he or she possesses the potential to have it even though it is not fully actualized. Similarly, the existence of persons with mental handicaps does not mean that rationality is not proper to human beings or that it cannot be predicated of disabled persons as a potency.

But what is an intersex condition? The Intersex Society of North America offers the following definition: "Intersex is a general term used for a variety of conditions in which a

---

[48]   Karol Wojtyla, *Love and Responsibility*, trans. H.T. Willets (San Francisco: Ignatius Press, 1993), 47.

person is born with a reproductive or sexual anatomy that doesn't seem to fit the typical definitions of female or male."[49] Examples of intersex conditions include: Androgyn Insensitivity Syndrome (complete or partial), clitoromegaly (large clitoris), Congenital Adrenal Hyperplasia (CAH), gonadal dysgenesis (partial and complete), micropenis, MRKH (congenital absence of a vagina), and Turner Syndrome. Estimates of the number of persons affected by such conditions can vary from 0.22% to 4.0% of the population.[50] The United Nations estimates the numbers to be between 0.5% and 1.7%.[51] The variance in numbers can be explained in part by the difficulty in obtaining agreement on what qualifies as an intersex condition. In other words, when does a small penis or a large clitoris become an intersex condition? The numbers can also be inflated by advocates of gender ideology for political purposes.

In the vast majority of intersex conditions, despite ambiguous expression of sexual difference in one or more of the dimensions of its biological expression (e.g., genital, gonadal, hormonal, chromosomal, secondary sex characteristics), it is possible to discern the person's bodily reality as belonging to one sex or the other. Dominican bioethicist Nicanor Austriaco proposes two tests in this regard: first, the

---

49   See the definition on the group's website, https://isna.org/faq/what_is_intersex/.
50   The 4.0% figure was first put forward by John Money and disseminated by Anne Fausto-Sterling. See "Intersex population figures," Intersex Human Rights Australia, https://ihra.org.au/16601/intersex-numbers/.
51   See the "Fact Sheet: Intersex," Free & Equal (A UN Group dedicated to LGBT rights), https://www.unfe.org/wp-content/uploads/2017/05/UNFE-Intersex.pdf.

ability to generate children as a man or woman (i.e., outside of or within the person's body; and second, engaging in the conjugal act as a man or a woman.[52] While the first of these is more determinative, given that some intersex conditions cause infertility, the second might be the only relevant consideration in some cases. Building on this analysis in light of John Paul II's Theology of the Body, Beth Lofgren argues that while the body speaks through the maleness or femaleness of a healthy person, in the case of an intersex person the body "whispers."[53] So it requires more attentive listening and discernment by those around the individual.

A few further observations about persons with intersex conditions are in order. First, despite efforts of proponents of gender ideology, many persons with intersex conditions do not consider themselves to be "transgender" and have little interest in our contemporary gender politics. They simply want to be able to live their lives. Second, while doctors used to try to aggressively "assign" a sex to intersex children early on through medical intervention in consultation with parents, it has become clear that this approach is flawed. Research indicates that such individuals do better if parents and medical professionals wait until adolescence or adulthood when the person can help to decide whether to have

[52]   See Nicanor Austriaco, O.P., "Specification of Sex/Gender in the Human Species: A Thomistic Analysis," *New Blackfriars* 94, no, 1054 (2013): 701-15.

[53]   "John Paul II's Theological Anthropology and the Intersexual Body," PhD Dissertation (Washington D.C.: The Catholic University of America, 2020). Lofgren's excellent study debunks the claim of Meghan DeFranza mentioned in the last chapter that the Theology of the Body cannot accommodate the reality of intersex conditions.

medical intervention, and, if so, what kind is appropriate.[54] Unlike the case of using gender transitioning procedures as a treatment for gender dysphoria, which is morally wrong and a form of mutilation, it can be completely appropriate for a mature individual with an intersex condition to seek medical assistance to clarify things like ambiguous genitalia or secondary sex characteristics. These instances of targeted surgery or hormone therapy are efforts by the person and his or her physicians to allow the sexed body to speak more clearly. Third, like all human beings, intersex persons are created for and fulfilled in the communion of love. Their bodily ambiguity can make this more difficult and may cause them to suffer. In most cases, however, it will not preclude them from marriage if they feel so called.[55] It in no way lessens their human dignity or value as persons created in the image of God and called to eternal life.

Reading the Body

When popes refer to the Church as "an expert in humanity," as Pope Sts. Paul VI and John Paul II did, it does not mean that she has an answer to every question about the human psyche or human sexuality. Some of those questions are scientific in nature and outside of the Church's competence to answer. We do not know what causes some people to be

---

[54]   See Peter A. Lee, Christopher P. Houk, S. Faisal Ahmed, Ieuan A. Hughes, "Consensus Statement on Management of Intersex Disorders," *Pediatrics*, 118, no. 2 (2006): e488–e500.

[55]   In the Church's understanding, infertility is not an impediment to marriage; however, impotence (i.e., the physical inability to engage in the conjugal act) is an impediment. See Canon 1084 of the *Code of Canon Law*.

attracted to members of their own sex rather than the opposite sex. There is evidence for both physical (e.g., genetic and neurohormonal) and developmental theories. If a consensus is someday reached, it will probably have to incorporate both nature and nurture in the explanation.[56] Whatever the causes of these conditions might be, they should not be understood as deterministic identities that override a person's moral freedom for his or her actions or behavior.

In regard to gender discordance or dysphoria, we do not have a complete picture either. As noted earlier, there are good reasons to see gender dysphoria as related to psychological disorders such as body dysmorphic disorder. There are other theories and explanations as well. Some have begun to argue for a physiological basis within the brain for this discordance—something like an intersex condition of the brain. The idea is interesting, but, thus far, compelling evidence for it is lacking. What is evident is that the aggressive medical intervention proposed by advocates of gender ideology does not reflect the best interests of patients or the ideals of medicine. The extensive chemical and surgical reconfiguration of the person's appearance often seems to leave the underlying psychological issues untouched and untreated. It is an undeniable fact that these procedures destroy the person's fertility—the capacity to be a physical mother or father. Catholic moral theology and healthcare can, therefore, only

---

[56] This is one of the conclusions of Nicanor Austriaco, O.P., "Understanding Sexual Orientation as a Habitus: Reasoning from the Natural Law, Appeals to Human Experience, and the Data of Science," in *Leaving and Coming Home: New Wineskins for Catholic Sexual Ethics*, ed. David Cloutier (Eugene, OR: Wipf & Stock, 2010), 101–18, see esp. 103.

view such procedures as a form of bodily mutilation and, thus, morally wrong.

Medieval theology spoke of two books—the book of nature and the book of Scripture. Both have God for their author and, therefore, when read rightly, do not contradict one another. Contrary to the currently popular view that faith and science are inescapably in tension, Christians have nothing to fear from science when it is grounded in reality. "Science" subordinated to and manipulated by philosophical or political commitments such as gender ideology is another matter. That so-called science and the medicine practiced in its name can do real and lasting harm to human beings.

Although the body may be likened to a compass, we need Scripture and Tradition to understand it and navigate by it. Human reason can see in the sexually differentiated bodies of men and women a natural teleology toward marriage, the complementarity involved in human procreation, and motherhood and fatherhood. Revelation completes the picture, giving a fuller picture of these truths as both natural realities and ones healed and elevated in the life of grace. Of course, it is only in the light of faith that we see the analogy between the communion of love in marriage and the family and the eternal communion of love among the Persons of the Blessed Trinity.

In his first encyclical, *Redemptor hominis*, John Paul II wrote: "Man cannot live without love. He remains a being that is incomprehensible for himself, his life is senseless, if love is not revealed to him, if he does not encounter love, if he does not experience it and make it his own, if he does not participate intimately in it."[57] The sexually differentiated body is a visible sign of this need for love: "It is not good for the man to be alone" (see Gn 2:18). It is also a sign of our vocation to communion—to the "sincere gift" of self in love. We are fulfilled only in communion and community with others. Yet, the fullness of the communion to which we are called transcends any merely human community. As the Council Fathers note: "Indeed, the Lord Jesus, when He prayed to the Father, 'that all may be one . . . as we are one' (Jn 17:21–22) opened up vistas closed to human reason, for He implied a certain likeness between the union of the divine Persons, and the unity of God's sons in truth and charity."[58] When God revealed Himself as a communion of Persons (Christ as Son of the Father and Bridegroom of the Church and the Holy Spirit proceeding from the Father and the Son), He in turn revealed the ultimate meaning of our existence as sexually differentiated persons: love—a love that will be fully realized in the Wedding Feast of the Lamb (cf. Rv 19:3–9; 21:1–4).

---

[57]   John Paul II, *Redemptor hominis*, no. 10.
[58]   *Gaudium et spes*, no. 24.

CHAPTER SEVEN

THE BATTLE AND BEYOND

"Shame and confusion! all is on the rout;
Fear frames disorder, and disorder wounds
Where it should guard. O war, thou son of hell,
Whom angry heavens do make their minister
Throw in the frozen bosoms of our part
Hot coals of vengeance! Let no soldier fly.
He that is truly dedicate to war
Hath no self-love, nor he that loves himself
Hath not essentially but by circumstance
The name of valour."
—Young Clifford, *Henry IV*, Part II

Tolerance is the virtue of the man without convictions.
—Gilbert K. Chesterton, *The Everlasting Man*

For a little space you may triumph on the field, for a day.
But against the Power that now arises there is no victory.
—Denethor, *The Return of the King*

In this book, we have followed the diagnosis of gender ideology laid out by Pope Benedict XVI in his final Christmas address to the Roman Curia in 2012. We looked at
what gender ideology is and its disturbing effects on marriage, the family, and society. Following the Holy Father's

lead, we looked at some of the sources of this ideology in modern feminism's turn to secular philosophies such as existentialism, post-modernism, and Marxism. We also considered how this ideology has spilled out into the wider culture through the ongoing dislocation of the family by the Industrial Revolution, the Sexual Revolution, and Technological Revolution. But the ultimate source of gender ideology is more ancient. It is a manifestation of the heresy of Gnosticism—perhaps the oldest and deadliest distortions of truth in Christian history—now clothed in modern garb. And Pope Benedict does not just offer a diagnosis—he points this heresy's cure. In the theology of creation described in the opening chapters of Genesis we can find a better account of the meaning of the body and sexual difference—one that can stand up to the light of both faith and human reason.

So where does this leave us in the current cultural battle going on around us?

"The Long Defeat"

Let us return once again to the powerful story told within the *Lord of the Rings*. While the arrival of Rohan along with aid from the south is enough to win a victory and prevent the fall of Minas Tirith, the respite is only temporary. The city's steward, Denethor, though himself in the grip of despair, prophetically declares to Gandalf at the height of the battle before the city gates: "For a little space you may triumph on the field, for a day. But against the Power that now arises there is no victory." Victory could not be achieved through force of arms, or the weapons of war—but only through humility, self-sacrifice, and the perseverance of the small and powerless against seemingly impossible odds. But even the climactic victory brought about by the destruction of the One Ring and the downfall of its maker Sauron only gives a temporary respite in a struggle against evil that stretches from the creation of the world to its apocalyptic conclusion. Tolkien's view of history that he carried into his mythology was shaped both by his work as a medievalist and by his own Catholic Faith. The struggle in Middle Earth against the powers of darkness and evil is described by Galadriel, the wise elven queen, as a largely futile task, an engagement in fighting "the long defeat."[1] In his letters, Tolkien ascribes this view directly to his Faith. In a letter written in 1956, he wrote: "Actually I am a Christian, and indeed a Roman Catholic, so that I do not expect 'history' to be anything but a 'long defeat'—though it contains (and in a legend may contain more clearly and movingly) some samples or glimpses of final victory."[2]

Why this somber excursion into Tolkien's Middle Earth at the outset and conclusion of this book? Aside from my own love for this particular mythology, I think that the allusions above bear some similarity to our own situation and afford an important perspective on it.

But isn't the language of "the long defeat"—for lack of a better word—defeatist? Understanding why the answer to this question is no requires some reflection on a Christian conception of history, the nature of salvation, and its bearing on human political life.

---

[1] Tolkien, *The Fellowship of the Ring* (New York: Ballantine Books, 1965), 462.
[2] Tolkien, "Letter," 195.

The current cultural battle against a toxic and highly secular gender ideology is but a contemporary manifestation of a much larger struggle that encompasses the whole of human history. This is a battle in which the force of weapons of war or other various human forms of power are useless. Ultimately, the battle is a spiritual one—a battle waged with weapons forged by truth and charity and sustained by the power of grace. And things like humility, self-sacrifice, and perseverance are enormously important in such combat. But this battle, no matter how valiantly fought, is nonetheless waged as part of "the long defeat." Human beings and even the Church herself cannot by themselves overcome the powers of evil arrayed against them. But they do not have to because victory is assured—and not just at a future eschatological finale to history. This victory has been accomplished in Christ's life, death, and Resurrection.

But, in God's plan of salvation, this victory requires the Cross. It cannot be won by the wielding of human power—whether military or political—that refuses the Cross. Jesus Himself faced this temptation in the desert (see Mt 4:1–11; esp. v. 9) and indeed throughout His ministry (see Mt 16:22–23). In his commentary on the Gospels, Pope Benedict XVI shows that this same temptation has been faced by the Church throughout her history, and it is faced in the life of each believer as well.[3] To share in Christ's victory, we must first be conformed to His Cross. It necessarily involves

---

[3]   See his analysis of Jesus' temptations in the desert in the second chapter of *Jesus of Nazareth: From the Baptism in the Jordan to the Transfiguration*, trans. Adrian J. Walker (New York: Image, 2007), 25–45.

opposition from and, at times, persecution by the powers that dominate our world; it involves fighting valiantly in the service of "the long defeat" before the final realization of the victory won on the Cross.

This is something consistently overlooked by Catholic integralists past and present who look to the state and its laws to impose true worship within political society.[4] They assume that Christ's reign through the Church is meant to be a political one just as many Jewish people of Jesus' day expected the Messiah to overthrow the Roman occupation of Palestine. But Jesus Himself denies that His Kingdom is to be found in this world (see Jn 18:36) and in John's Gospel the throne from which He reigns is the Cross itself. Historically, the Church has not fared well when she has been too closely identified with particular states and has attempted to wield political power within society.

Furthermore, no human inventions, including those which come from scientific or technological progress, can eradicate suffering and evil on the earth. Ideologies that claim to bring heaven to earth—especially apart from God—can only deceive. In his encyclical letter on Christian hope, *Spe salve*, Pope Benedict XVI contrasts the "faith in progress" of the modern world with authentic Christian hope. Progress in science and technology have given rise to the expectation in many circles that various kinds of suffering and evil can be overcome by human effort and ingenuity. Science displaces

---

[4] For a brief overview of current Catholic integralism and some of its flaws, see Steven Millies, "What is Catholic integralism?" *U.S. Catholic* (October 14, 2019), https://uscatholic.org/articles/2019 10/what-is-catholic-integralism/.

faith as the path to salvation: "Now, this 'redemption,' the restoration of the lost 'Paradise,' is no longer expected from faith but from the newly discovered link between science and praxis. It is not that faith is simply denied; rather it is displaced onto another level—that of purely private and other-worldly affairs—and, at the same time, it becomes somehow irrelevant for the world."[5]

The program proposed by gender ideology represents one instantiation of this modern form of Gnostic salvation, claiming to free individuals from the constraints of identity imposed by the body and nature. Christian hope, by contrast, places its confidence in God's providential direction of history according to His plan. This is why, Benedict says, the Last Judgment, rightly understood, is a setting for practicing hope.[6] As human beings, we do not have to right every wrong, cure every ill, or overcome every error. We do not have to save the world because, in truth, we cannot even save ourselves. In the end, "it is not science that redeems man: man is redeemed by love."[7]

The Limits of Tolerance

But why use the language of a battle at all? Does this not make unnecessarily adversarial what should be a civil conversation between different approaches to truth and the common good? After all, the Church sees no conflict between faith and reason, or between science and theology. There is one truth apprehended in these various disciplines.

---

5   Benedict XVI, *Spe salve* (November 30, 3007), no. 17.
6   See Ibid., nos. 41–48.
7   Ibid., no. 26.

The book of nature and the book of Scripture have but one Author. Should we not focus on mutual coexistence and tolerance in our pluralistic society?

There are multiple reasons why the language of a battle in the debate over sexual difference is not misplaced. It is certainly true that there is no conflict between the claims of faith and those of science when it comes to seeing and describing the reality of the world around us. But when science oversteps its bounds and purports to offer answers to the ultimate questions of happiness or salvation, especially in the service of an ideological program, then this pseudo-science has lost sight of its own nature and mission. Such ideological weaponization of science deserves to be exposed and opposed. As Benedict XVI observes, science is not a path to salvation.

Furthermore, given the aggressive social, educational, and legal policies described previously, it is clear that proponents of gender ideology are not interested in tolerance and coexistence. Clearly, the Judeo-Christian view of the sexually differentiated body having an inherent meaning and telos, ordering it to marriage, motherhood, and fatherhood, challenges gender ideology. It contradicts the narrative that one's body can be a constraint on personal realization or is merely a surface on which to write a gendered identity. These two views are radically opposed to one another and cannot both be true. This why proponents of gender ideology seek to label Christian views of the body, marriage, and sex as offensive or hateful and banish them from public expression—with the force of law when possible and with the force of ostracism when not.[8]

Conversely, neither can Christians leave the ideas advanced by gender ideology unchallenged. This book has argued that gender ideology is a twenty-first century expression of Gnosticism—one flavored by secular currents of modern thought such as existentialism, postmodernism, and Marxism, and enabled by the social dislocation caused by recent cultural shifts. As a current expression of Gnosticism, it is a heresy. It offers a false conception of the body, sexual difference, and the path to authentic human flourishing and happiness. Its ideas need to be exposed as untrue and defeated intellectually within the Church and in the public square. The Church Fathers saw opposing and defeating heresy within the Christian community and refuting false philosophies as being integral to the Christian apologetics that must accompany the preaching of the gospel.[9] This apologetic effort is not foreign to Christian charity—it is an instantiation and extension of it. We love because we have first been loved (see

---

[8]   On this zeal to eradicate Christian sexual views from the public arena, see David Carlin, "Our Sexual Carthage Must Be Destroyed," The Catholic Thing, April 22, 2016, https://www.thecat holicthing.org/2016/04/22/our-sexual-carthage-must-be-destro yed/.

[9]   This is not to say that all human philosophies are untrue or incompatible with revelation. Many of the Fathers drew on Stoic and Neo-Platonic ideas, which they saw as harmonious with Christian teaching. Augustine compares Christians taking truths from secular philosophy and literature and using them in the service of the gospel to the Israelites despoiling the Egyptians of their treasures in Exodus 12. See Augustine, *De doctrina christiana* II, 40.

1 Jn 4:19) and so offer to others the life-giving truth that has been given to us.

The opponents in this battle are not people who identify as LGBTQ+ or even the most ardent proponents of gender ideology—it is the ideas themselves and the falsehoods they contain. Unmasking these falsehoods for what they are is part of the spiritual combat that comprises the Christian life (see Eph 6:10–17). We are called to confront and oppose evil and falsehood within ourselves and within the world around us. As St. Paul wrote, defending his own apostolic authority and teaching: "For, although we are in the flesh, we do not battle according to the flesh, for the weapons of our battle are not of flesh but are enormously powerful, capable of destroying fortresses. We destroy arguments and every pretension raising itself against the knowledge of God, and take every thought captive in obedience to Christ" (2 Cor 10:3–5). Toleration of false anthropologies or accounts of salvation is therefore not an option for those seeking to practice Christian charity.

A Different Kind of War; Different Kinds of Weapons

If the Church takes sides in what some have called "the culture wars," she therefore does so not for political purposes or to win victories in the public arena of opinions and ideas. She does so as part of her own mission of evangelization. She does so to do her part in valiantly fighting "the long defeat." She does so in fidelity to her crucified Lord. As St. Teresa of Calcutta famously observed, the Lord has called us to be "faithful, not successful."[10]

Rightly understood, Catholic teaching cuts across our current political divides and ideologies and should not be read as "liberal" or "conservative." These labels refer to political ideas and fashions that have changed over time. The "economic liberalism" of eighteenth and nineteenth-century thinkers such as Adam Smith and T. R. Malthus, defending market-based economics, is in today's parlance identified in the West as economic conservatism.[11] Catholic theology and teaching aims not at conforming to changing political fashions or ideologies—it aims at truth and orthodoxy.[12] In fact, Catholic teaching tends to fall on the "liberal" side of contemporary American politics on issues such as social and economic justice, the environment, and immigration. Conversely, it tends to be seen as "conservative" on issues of life, marriage, and sexuality. But this teaching is a coherent,

---

[10]   Former U.S. Senator Mark Hatfield tells of visiting the "Home for the Dying" run by the Missionaries of Charity in 1976. The Senator asked Mother Teresa, "How can you bear the load without being crushed beneath it?" To which she said, "My dear Senator, I am not called to be successful, I am called to be faithful." See Art Beals, *Beyond Hunger: A Biblical Mandate for Social Responsibility* (Colorado Springs, CO: Multinomah Press, 1985).

[11]   Thus, Vittorio Messori said of then Cardinal Ratzinger that from the perspective of his deep religious faith, "all those schematic formulations *conservative/progressive, right/left* which stem from an altogether different sphere, namely, that of political ideologies, lose their meaning." *The Ratzinger Report: An Exclusive Interview on the State of the Church* (San Francisco: Ignatius, 1985), 12 (emphasis in original).

[12]   See Ratzinger and Messori, *The Ratzinger Report*, 23.

unified whole grounded in an understanding of human nature and the dignity of human persons.[13]

This book's treatment of sexual difference and the dangers of "gender ideology" is not an attempt to take sides in "the culture wars" that have occupied much of American social and political life. If Christians join these battles they do so because their faith moves them, the same way it moves them to defend the unborn, to work for racial justice, or to protect the environment. They may well work side by side for these goals with people of other faiths or no religious faith. But they do so with an allegiance to a different King and with a different vision, shaped by an understanding of history that sees the Cross as its center. And they do so as part of a larger spiritual battle that encompasses the whole of human life and history. They do so in the hope of inviting others to encounter the Person of Jesus Christ Who is the center and Lord of human history. It is but the current chapter of "the long defeat," and it is ours to write as we strive to be faithful while awaiting the final victory that is ultimately the work of God.

The weapons of this battle are not those of war or of political power. They are weapons of truth, love, and the grace of the Holy Spirit wielded through humility and self-sacrifice. Among these weapons, one of the most important is mercy. Pope Francis draws our attention to the teaching of St. Thomas Aquinas. For Thomas, the most perfect

---

[13]   For an excellent analysis of Catholic teaching as transcending the conservative/liberal divide and grounded in human dignity, see Erika Bachiochi, "Reflections on the Kinship between Catholic Sexual and Social Teaching," in *Women, Sex, and the Church: A Case for Catholic Teaching*, Erika Bachiochi, ed. (Boston: Daughters of St. Paul, 2010), 179–92.

manifestation of the grace of the Holy Spirit within the moral life of the Christian is the exercise of the virtue of mercy: "In itself mercy is the greatest of the virtues, since all the others revolve around it and, more than this, it makes up for their deficiencies. This is particular to the superior virtue, and as such it is proper to God to have mercy, through which his omnipotence is manifested to the greatest degree."[14] Elsewhere, the Holy Father connects this virtue to God Himself, writing in his bull announcing the Jubilee Year of mercy: "Jesus Christ is the face of the Father's mercy. These words might well sum up the mystery of the Christian faith. Mercy has become living and visible in Jesus of Nazareth, reaching its culmination in him."[15] In Christ, we encounter the Father who is "rich in mercy" (Eph 2:4). This mercy, he tells us later in the same document, is "the beating heart of the gospel."[16] Like charity, mercy is what we ourselves receive from God, and that which makes us like Him. Having been touched and changed by that mercy, we are impelled to invite others to the same life-changing experience.

Confronting and defeating gender ideology's distorted "theology" is in the service of inviting others to experience God's mercy and love for them. The body and its sex are not limits to be overcome in writing a personal identity or prisons to be escaped through technology; they are visible signs of a call to communion of love and life. Pope Francis

---

14   Aquinas, *Summa Theologiae* II-II, q. 30, a. 4, cited in Francis, "Apostolic Exhortation *Evangelii Gaudium* (November 24, 2013), no. 37.

15   Francis, Bull of Indiction, *Misericordiae vultus* (April 11, 2015), no. 1.

16   Ibid., no. 12.

has called the Church to a "missionary conversion" in all of Her activity and structures.[17] In this vein, apologetics and public debates ought to be shaped by evangelical mercy. This was the understanding of the Church Fathers and the great scholastic theologians of the Middle Ages—it needs to be ours as well.

The Field Hospital of the Church

Pope Francis has also called for the virtue of mercy to permeate the presentation of the Church's moral teaching. Recalling the imagery of the woman caught in adultery in chapter eight of John's Gospel, he warns against those who: "Rather than offering the healing power of grace and the light of the Gospel message . . . would 'indoctrinate' that message, turning it into 'dead stones to be hurled at others.'"[18] The Church's moral teaching is not meant to be weaponized against those inside or outside of it. It is meant to be heard as an invitation to mercy and life.

This does not mean, as some have concluded, that there is no such thing as sin or that we should not talk about the reality of sin in the name of a generic and misplaced appeal to pastoral mercy. If there is no such thing as sin, then the mercy of God so boundlessly demonstrated on the Cross loses its meaning (see Rom 5:8). Sin is real, and its effects are devastating. And sin is an equal opportunity despot that seeks to rule us all as St. Paul declares in his Letter to the Romans, describing the lot of Jews and Gentiles alike: "For there is no distinction; all have sinned and are deprived of

---

[17]   Francis, *Evangelii gaudium*, nos. 25–27.
[18]   Francis, *Amoris laetitia*, no. 49.

the glory of God" (3:22–23). We cannot accuse others while we excuse ourselves. Scripture and Pope Francis warn us against this kind of judgment (see Lk 6:37).

In a thoughtful essay, Michael W. Hannon has warned against turning sexual desires into identities or orientations—whether homosexual or heterosexual.[19] This "orientation essentialism" "binds" same-sex attracted people to their sins and denies their Christian freedom, effectively telling them that their desires are their destiny. It likewise "blinds" opposite-sex attracted people to their own disordered desires as they get to hide behind a quasi-scientific patina of "normal" sexuality. Although focused on sexual attraction versus sexual difference and identity, Hannon's cautions are instructive for people dealing with gender dysphoria or discordance. They remind us that the call to conversion articulated by Catholic moral teaching is directed to everyone without exception—same-sex attracted, opposite-sex attracted, gender discordant, and those secure in their gender identities.

Not everyone who experiences same-sex attraction, gender discordance, or struggles with the pain of gender dysphoria subscribes to gender ideology or self identifies as LGBTQ+, but these persons are particularly susceptible to getting conscripted by gender ideology in one of its many forms. It is in encountering, listening to, accompanying, and befriending such people that Pope Francis's warning

---

[19]   See Michael W. Hannon, "Against Heterosexuality," First Things, no. 241 (March 1, 2014): https://www.firstthings.com/article/20 14/03/against-heterosexuality. Since writing that piece Hannon has entered religious life and is now known as Fr. Urban Hannon.

against weaponizing doctrine and reminders about the centrality of mercy in the Christian life are especially relevant and important. Reflecting the face of God to these souls is precisely what Pope Francis recommends to those Christians who would be "missionary disciples" in the world today.[20] It is not accidental that this is a decidedly person-centered and incarnational approach to evangelization, as opposed to the "drive by" approaches prevalent in media, social media, or large religious gatherings. This model has particular importance for ministering to people who are same-sex attracted or gender discordant since they often feel unheard and rejected by family and perhaps their religious communities.

At the beginning of his pontificate, Pope Francis gave an interview in which he compared the Church to a field hospital:[21]

> The thing the church needs most today is the ability to heal wounds and to warm the hearts of the faithful; it needs nearness, proximity. I see the church as a field hospital after battle. It is useless to ask a seriously injured person if he has high cholesterol and about the level of his blood sugars! You have to heal his wounds. Then we can talk about everything else. Heal the wounds, heal the wounds. . . . And you have to start from the ground up.[22]

---

[20] See Francis, *Evangelii gaudium*, nos. 169–71.

[21] It is worth noting that a field hospital is always found in proximity to a battle.

[22] Antonio Spadaro, S.J., "A Big Heart Open to God: An Interview with Pope Francis," *America Magazine* September 19, 2013, https://www.americamagazine.org/faith/2013/09/30/big-heart-open-god-interview-pope-francis.

In the same interview, the pope emphatically described himself as a sinner: "I am a sinner. This is the most accurate
definition. It is not a figure of speech, a literary genre. I am
a sinner." Putting the two ideas together, Pope Francis suggests that the Church is the hospital where sinners (i.e., all
of us) have their wounds treated by Christ, the Great Physician. In seeking to accompany and evangelize others we act
as orderlies of the Great Physician, inviting others to "come,
and you will see" (Jn 1:39) the mercy and healing we ourselves have experienced.

These images are not new in the tradition. Saint Augustine too frequently refers to Christ as the Great Physician.
Thus, he says, "The Lord, though, like an experienced doctor, knew better what was going on in the sick man, than
the sick man himself. Doctors do for the indispositions of
bodies what the Lord can also do for the indisposition of
souls."[23] And, for the Bishop of Hippo, the hospital used by
this Divine Doctor is the Church: "Let us, the wounded,
entreat the physician, let us be carried to the inn to be
healed . . . therefore Brothers, in this time the Church too,
in which the wounded man is healed, is the inn of the trav-
eler."[24] For St. Augustine the parable of the Good Samaritan
is an allegory of the story of salvation. Each one of us is the
wounded person set upon and left for dead by sin and the

---

[23]   Augustine, *Sermon*, 2290. The citation is from The Works of St.
Augustine: A Translation for the 21st Century, Sermons III/6
(184–229Z), trans. Edmund Hill, O.P., ed. John Rotelle, O.S.A.
(New City: New York, 1993), 323.

[24]   Augustine, *Tractates on the Gospel of John*, 41.13.2. The citation is
from *Saint Augustine Tractates on the Gospel of John* 28–54, trans.
John W. Rettig (Washington: CUA Press, 1993), 148–49.

devil. Each one of us is left by the side of the road by the law and religious ritual apart from the life of grace. Each one of us is treated by Christ who pours on our wounds the oil and wine of the sacraments made available through His Cross, carried to the "inn" of the Church for convalescence and left with the down payment of the Holy Spirit until the Samaritan's return.

Building on the gift of creation, the Christian story of salvation provides a narrative for human identity far deeper than a self-articulated and technologically fabricated construct. It tells us that each embodied human person is chosen and loved by God from all eternity. It tells us, in the memorable phrase of Pope St. John Paul II, that the body is fundamentally "a witness to love" and that its maleness and femaleness are an integral part of that witness.[25] Sexual difference is also integral to the person's capacity to give him or herself as a gift through the body: whether in marriage and parenthood, consecrated life or religious celibacy, Christian single life in the world, or in the ultimate gift of martyrdom. To imitate Christ crucified, each person must give him or herself away in love as a man or woman, holding nothing back from Him who held nothing back from His Church. And, as Pope Benedict XVI said in his last public address before his retirement: "One receives one's life precisely when one offers it as a gift."[26] By taking on a sexually differentiated human body, Christ elevated our human nature and revealed that gender is a gift not to be destroyed, manipulated, or redefined; rather, our bodies are good gifts

---

[25]   John Paul II, *Man and Woman*, 14:5, 183.
[26]   Benedict XVI, General Audience, February 27, 2013.

are meant to be offered back to the Father. And those who suggest otherwise preach a false gospel, an ancient heresy. But those who embrace the true gospel hold that everything God made is good, especially our male and female bodies, which are meant to be temples of the Holy Spirit.